ITINERANT
PHOTOGRAPHER
Corpus Christi, 1934

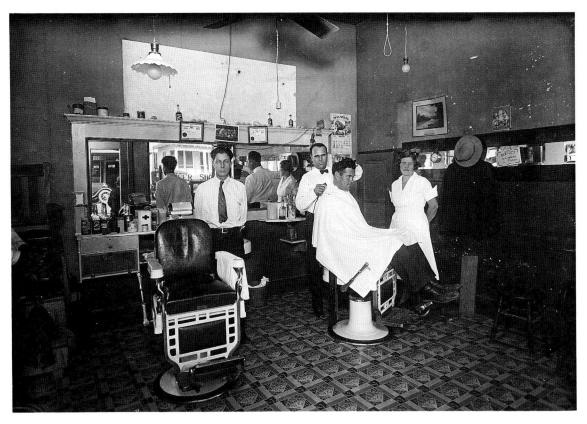

Unidentified Barber Shop.

ITINERANT PHOTOGRAPHER

Corpus Christi, 1934

Sybil Miller

Afterword by
Bill Stott

University of New Mexico Press
ALBUQUERQUE

Library of Congress Cataloging-in-
Publication Data

Miller, Sybil, 1956–
  Itinerant photographer.

  Bibliography: p.
  1. Corpus Christi (Tex.)
—Description—Views. 2. Corpus
Christi (Tex.)—Social life and
customs—Pictorial works.
3. Photography—Texas—Corpus
Christi—History—20th century.
I. Title.
F394.C78M55 1987   779'.99764113
86-24948
ISBN 0-8263-0935-6 (pbk.)

Contents

Acknowledgments

Research on obscure photographers and little-known areas in the history of photography is never easy. This book would not have been possible without the generous help and support of many individuals and institutions in Corpus Christi and elsewhere in Texas, and across the country.

Most important to this project was the essential support and assistance of Dr. John F. "Doc" McGregor. Doc McGregor must be credited with the great foresight of saving the itinerant's relatively unimportant glass-plate negatives. In addition, McGregor energetically made his own photographs of Corpus Christi and its residents, resulting in a visual portrait of south Texas that spans over fifty years. The McGregor archive, now housed both at the University of Texas at Austin and in Corpus Christi, totals nearly a half million negatives and prints. I sincerely hope that this important photographic and historical record will be given the attention it so much deserves.

I also wish to acknowledge the invaluable help of Doc McGregor's daughter, Lorena Jean Tinker. Lorena first pointed out to me that the photographs in this book were not taken by her father, but were instead the work of an itinerant. She was always extremely helpful as I worked on my project, many times taking time away from her own research to help me with mine.

Many people in Corpus Christi generously helped me during the past five years. I especially want to thank Margaret Walberg for her unfailing support, enthusiasm, and hospitality, and for bringing me into contact with long-time residents of Corpus Christi who shared their memories and their homes with me during my many trips to their city. Lee John Govatos, son of the Pier Cafe's owner John Govatos, was the first person I met in Corpus Christi and from that day on was always more than willing to help in every way. For their generous assistance, I am also grateful to J. B. Adams, Frank Allen, Judge Robert Barnes, Mrs. Dave Berlin, J. Richard Bluntzer, Col. Floyd Buch, Raymond Carr, Hazel Crocker, Lee Crocker, Floyd Crow, Charles Davis, Antonio Garcia, Ray Garcia, Mrs. William H. Gentry, William Green, Victor Herold, Charlie Hrissikopoulos, Mr. and Mrs. Arthur Ilse, Bill Jones, W. W. Jones, Joe Kanipe, Dan Kilgore, Mr. and Mrs. J. T. King, Mr. and Mrs. Ray Kring, Mamie Lambert, Lester Luehrs, Mrs. Ward McCampbell, Mr. and Mrs. Arthur McGregor, Shirley Paul Mireur, Erma Catherine Biel Morley, George Munson, Thomas Murphy, Charlie Murray, William Neyland, Jr., Mr. and Mrs. Gus Nicols, Lou Oliver, John Padilla, Thelma Gollihar Peterson, Harry Pinson, Alclaire Pleasant, George, Olga, and Harry Plomarity, Elsie Poenisch, Mr. and Mrs. Everett L. Powell, Mr. and Mrs. Lonnie Price, Mrs. Fred Quaille, Margaret Ramage, Don Riggs, Sally Robeau, Laura Rodriguez, Beulah Scogin, Buster Shely, Jack Sloma, Farrell Smith, Marie Steurer, Jack Taylor, Marion Uehlinger, Bill Warren, C. B. Weil, and L. L. Woodman. I also want to thank Jewell Tallmadge, George Tallmadge, Jr., George Tallmadge, III, and John Talmadge [sic] for helping me trace George Tallmadge, Sr., and his role in the itinerant's pictures.

Also in Corpus Christi, the Nueces County Historical Society and the Friends of the Courthouse were most helpful in sponsoring an exhibit and symposium on the McGregor Collection, held in the Commissioner's Courtroom of the Nueces County Courthouse and funded in part by the Texas Committee for the Humanities. The local history room of the La Retama Library was often a source of both refuge and information during my trips to Corpus Christi. The staff there has assembled an excellent archive of materials I could find nowhere else.

I began work on the photographs in the McGregor Collection while a graduate student in the American Civilization program at the University of Texas at Austin. Many people at the university encouraged and discussed my project with me, most importantly Dr. Joe B. Frantz, Dr. William Goetzman, and Dr. Jeffrey Meikle. Special thanks go to Roy Flukinger, curator of the Harry Ransom Humanities Research Center's Photography Collection, who has supported this project from the beginning, and to the staff at the collection, in particular May Ellen MacNamara, whose long-time interest in regional Texas photography was always encouraging. Eric Beggs also deserves special mention; he made many of the prints reproduced here, going out of his way to print "unprintable" glass plates.

Eugene O. Goldbeck played an especially important role in this project. Without his early experience as an itinerant photographer, much of the information in this book would be founded on little more than my speculation. Goldbeck generously shared his recollections and greatly enriched my research and understanding of photography.

For their generous assistance in helping me locate additional examples of itinerant photography and much important information on itinerant photographers, I am grateful to the following institutions and individuals: Byron Johnson and the Albuquerque Museum, Heather Hatch and the Arizona Historical Society, the Austin History Center, the Barker Texas History Center, Carlen Luke and the California Historical Society, Michelle Campbell, William S. Bunchuck and CBS Magazines, Amy Stark and the Center for Creative Photography, Joe Coltharp, the Library of Congress, Martha Utterback and Berenice Strong at the Daughters of the Republic of Texas, Texas History Research Library, Mary Sarber and the El Paso Public Library, Wayne Daniel and the Ft. Concho Museum, Shirley Goodman, Libby Barker and the Hemphill County Library, Thomas Kreneck and the Houston Metropolitan Research Center at the Houston Public Library, Maria Gonzalez and the Indiana Historical Society Library, the Library at the International Museum of Photography/George Eastman House, David Haynes and the Institute of Texas Cultures, Russell Lee, Gary Yarrington and the Lyndon Baines Johnson Library-Museum, L. L. McCall, Tracy Baker and the Minnesota Historical Society, Dale Monaghen, the Montana Historical Society, John E. Carter and Marilyn Stuart and the Nebraska State Historical Society, Arthur L. Olivas and the Museum of New Mexico, Helena Zinkham and the New York Historical Society, the Municipal Archives of the City of New York, the National Archives, Lorraine Patteson Nichols, Susan Seyl and the Oregon Historical Society, Peter Palmquist, the Panhandle-Plains Museum, Kim Ross, Herb Sculnick, the Shugart Studio, Hilda Bohem and the University of California, Los Angeles, Bobbi Klepler and the University of Texas-Permian Basin, Mrs. Eric Warren, and Myrna Williamson and the State Historical Society of Wisconsin.

Paul Vanderbilt deserves special thanks for his help at the State Historical Society of Wisconsin. Paul's work at the SHSW archive is immensely important, and his commitment to the value of regional photography sets a standard that other state and local archives should follow.

My appreciation goes to Carole Kismaric at Aperture for first publishing a selection of the itinerant's pictures in Aperture #90. Her early recognition of the significance of these photographs was a great encouragement.

The manuscript of this book has greatly benefited from the suggestions of Marianne Fulton, associate curator at the International Museum of Photography/George Eastman House. Bill Stott read numerous drafts of my master's thesis and then my manuscript with great care and patience. His suggestions are gratefully acknowledged, as are his insights into the Depression era and the Corpus Christi photographs. I would also like to thank Dana Asbury for her sensitive editing of the final draft.

I especially wish to thank Richard Rudisill for his encouragement and interest in my project and for bringing it to the attention of the UNM Press. Richard's interest in the early stages of my research was most encouraging.

Many friends contributed their help in various ways during the past five years. Barbara McCandless accompanied me on several research trips and offered constant encouragement and, on occasion, much needed sympathy. Richard Pearce-Moses loaned me his computer, saving me from weeks of frustration, and many times directed me to obscure archives that proved invaluable. Victoria Smith encouraged me throughout the project and proved handy at assembling mats and typing captions. And Rixon Reed offered me flexible employment at Photo-Eye Books, always giving me time for traveling and writing, something that only an employer who is also a friend would do. Each of them made significant contributions to my project, and this book owes a great deal to them.

When I think of all that is involved in researching historical photographs—the expense of numerous research trips and the demands on one's time—it seems an impossible undertaking without the unqualified support of one's family. My husband, Mark Goodman, always offered his encouragement and spent many hours discussing my project as it progressed. His belief in the value of regional, vernacular photography made it possible for me to recognize the importance of the itinerant's photographs when I first saw them. Since then, he has been more than patient and understanding during the many times when my research took precedence over other responsibilities. But this entire project would not have been possible without the support of my parents, Dr. and Mrs. Maurice Miller. Since I first went to Corpus Christi in 1981, they always helped in any way they could, at any time, from assembling frames for an exhibit to making it possible for me to travel and work without institutional support or outside funding. This book is for them.

Introduction

In early 1934, Corpus Christi, Texas, was a fairly active small city, prosperous and optimistic compared to communities hit harder by the Great Depression. In February, a transient came to town, just as transients drift to the south Texas coast every winter, but this man was different. He carried a camera, wore a suit, and asked for no hand-outs. While he was not an aimless drifter or tramp, neither did he envision himself a documentor of his times, as did the nineteenth-century Nebraska photographer Solomon Butcher, for no historically minded photographer would abandon such a valuable archive. The Corpus Christi photographer was simply a working man who carried his trade with him and lived on the fringes of society while photographing doctors, lawyers, judges, and those with less prestigious occupations. He was an itinerant photographer with apparently no ambition beyond getting to the next town, but as the photographs in this book reveal, one with impressive skills.

During the Depression even successful studio photographers found themselves in financial trouble, and itinerant photographers, like their contemporaries the Bible salesmen, knew that their livelihood depended on surefire sales techniques. Itinerant photographers were often called "kidnappers," a term that originally applied to door-to-door baby photographers. Making his way through a residential area, leading a pony, the kidnapper would introduce himself to the housewife, flash a few prints he had made of other children, and declare he wanted to photograph the woman's children—no charge, no obligation. A few days later, the kidnapper returned offering the image he had made for "ransom." Parental

George Tallmadge, ca. 1965, San Marcos, Texas. (Courtesy Jewell Tallmadge and George Tallmadge, III.)

pride usually ensured a sale. Eventually the term kidnapper came to be applied to all photographers with this calculated sales approach, including some who photographed passersby on street corners and specialists who made the rounds of shops and businesses, like the Corpus Christi photographer. While to us today the word may seem quaint, in the 1930s *kidnapper* was a derogatory term used by studio photographers aiming to discredit itinerants, their greatest competition.

Almost nothing is known about this particular photographer in Corpus Christi, and no new information is likely to be uncovered. Of the hundreds of people he photographed in that month in Corpus Christi, only one subject can remember him—Lonnie Price, then a bellhop at the Plaza Hotel (Plate 110). Price recalls only having had his picture taken by "a transient—a photographer off the street," wearing a suit.

Itinerants often traveled by themselves, but some worked as a team with an assistant, a "proof-passer" who would return the second day to show the proofs and sell prints, while the photographer continued photographing more businesses. In Corpus Christi, the itinerant seems to have worked with George Tallmadge, a local photographer who had a studio in the central business district—an ideal location for a kidnapper's headquarters. Tallmadge's business had not been doing well, so he may have welcomed the opportunity for additional income. The itinerant may have arranged for Tallmadge to work as his darkroom man and possibly

proof-passer as well, or he may have simply rented Tallmadge's darkroom facilities and hired another assistant. Whatever the case, when the itinerant moved on he left his 560 glass plates with Tallmadge as part of the deal.

A year or so later, Tallmadge transferred his studio to Pearsall, Texas; in the early 1940s, he moved again to San Marcos, Texas, where his business thrived until the 1960s. (Sadly, no archive of his work survives today, except for scattered prints in family albums.) When he left Corpus Christi, he realized the itinerant's glass plates were of no commercial value outside the city, so Tallmadge passed them on to his friend Dr. John F. "Doc" McGregor.

"Doc" McGregor, a chiropractor whose interest in photography overtook his medical career, is known today as Corpus Christi's premier photographer, a shutterbug who became as well known to local residents as some of those he photographed (including President Franklin Delano Roosevelt on a fishing trip in nearby Port Aransas). In the mid-1930s, Doc's photography career was well under way. Like Tallmadge, he had no use for the itinerant's negatives, but simply to discard them went against his nature. Instead, he stored them until his retirement in 1976, when he donated them to the Photography Collection at the University of Texas at Austin. (The bulk of McGregor's own work, over a half million negatives and prints, is in the Corpus Christi Museum). Recognizing their significance, Joe Coltharp, curator at the collection, had a set of study prints made from the plates, and Eric Warren, former resident of Corpus Christi, along with Austin photographer Ave Bonar set about the immense task of identifying the people and places in the pictures. Absolutely no information on either photographer or subject came with the glass plates, no list of names or receipt book. That the pictures are so well captioned is a tribute to the remarkable eye and memory of Eric Warren.

When we think of the 1930s, we tend to think only of the poor and the dispossessed—the men, women, and children forced to migrate by economic and natural disasters. Certainly many of the people who lived through the thirties experienced the hardships of the Depression, but there were other sides to life in Corpus Christi. The itinerant's photographs offer a glimpse of the people who remained employed during the Depression, working in ordinary and typical businesses: beauty and barber shops, cafés, grocery stores, bars, offices—the public places that formed an important part of daily life.

Professors, Itinerants, and Kidnappers

In February of 1934, an itinerant photographer made nearly five hundred pictures of businessmen, professionals, storekeepers, government employees, and laborers in Corpus Christi, Texas. With his 5×7 glass-plate camera and flashpowder equipment, he canvassed the business districts, making wide-angle views of these people in their working environments. Making his pictures on speculation, not commission, he was not employed by the local Chamber of Commerce, by a state or federal agency, or by any other group or organization. He was an independent journeyman—part speculator, part craftsman, part con artist.

While the Corpus Christi pictures may seem new and strange to our eyes, at one time they were as common to photography as the department store portrait is today. This itinerant did not "invent" a new way of seeing and in fact worked within a well-established pictorial genre, although one that has gone unrecognized in previous histories of photography. Two things make this photographer stand out. First, his photographs are unusual because they exist as a group of intact negatives from a single time and place. I know of only a few other collections similar to this and none are as large or cohesive.[1] Second, this itinerant, although primarily concerned with earning a living, made exceptionally good use of his camera and lens, producing a large group of pictures of excellent (and sometimes extraordinary) quality.

When I first saw these photographs, I was naturally curious about their maker. While some argue that the interpretation of photographs should not depend on what we know of the photographer, I believe that a picture's content is as firmly linked to its maker as it is to its subject and cultural context. When looking at photographs, the more you know about both photographer and subject, the more you see. When I learned that the Corpus Christi itinerant was anonymous, I immediately began searching for his identity. I found that he left behind no records of his business dealings in Corpus Christi; no receipt book or list of prospective clients exists today. More surprising, I learned that he sold his prints unsigned and without a commercial stamp bearing his name or address. I could not associate any name with the photographs, much less determine the photographer's social background or personal history.

With other bodies of work we can look to the photographer for clues to the photographs; in this case we must look to the photographs for clues to the photographer. It is necessary to look beyond this to the written accounts, few and slim as they are, of other itinerants throughout the nineteenth and twentieth centuries to help construct a context for these pictures. Through such accounts and the photographs themselves, a history of itinerant photography in America begins to emerge and with it the Corpus Christi itinerant.

In 1931 an itinerant photographer based in Oklahoma, E. F. Cordell, made his way to the new oil fields in east Texas. *Pittman's Trade Tips*, a photography trade bulletin published in Dallas, wrote of Cordell: "When a new field opens he gets an 'itch' in the feet that is only satisfied when he gets located in the center of activities."[2] This "itch" to travel, to seek out exciting places and people, was certainly not new in 1931 nor peculiar to Cordell, although recent improvements in roads and automobiles made satisfying the urge to travel a more comfortable and less risky venture.

In his book *The Mirror Image*, historian Richard Rudisill sees the itinerant daguerreotypist as a "compass needle to the restless expansive pull of American life."[3] Rudisill feels that these photographers traveled under the influence of "the westering impulse and the general mood of manifest destiny."[4] Caught up by the pioneer spirit and attracted by the economic opportunities in newly settled areas, the early itinerants "wandered freely over the land, sometimes with a goal in mind, more often with only the drive of a restless age urging them along."[5] This initial urge for travel continued throughout the nineteenth century and into the twentieth, while the frontier shifted from a physical reality to a psychological longing.

Itinerant photographers did not take up a profession so much as they chose a life-style, and many photographers used the camera as a means to travel, escape a boring job, and seek adventure. In the 1920s, the itinerant postcard photographer Paul Holt found the marriage of photography and the road so perfect that he was moved to write a how-to book for other dissatisfied souls, *$50 a Week with Camera and Car* (1926). In this little guide Holt candidly states his desire for freedom: "All of us have a longing to be gypsies at times, to break away from our bondage to mere things, to leave our prisons of brick and brownstone fronts, and to face the World of Adventure as Free Men."[6]

Holt's ideals are similar to those fostered by artists and intellectuals of the twenties who embraced the Romantic notion of achieving personal integrity by rejecting conventional life-styles and remaining independent of American business society.[7] Instead of pursuing financial success and domestic stability, Holt exalts a life of risk, individuality, and mobility. The camera, as a source of income, is merely a means to this end.

When Holt took to the road, he was a recent college graduate, "unfitted for any particular work"—a young rebel who "hated to go to work in an office or store for 8 or 9 hours for somebody else."[8] He traveled about the country making postcards of homes in middle-class neighborhoods of medium-sized cities. He lived and worked out of his car, reducing his expenses to a minimum. In fact, on a typical day he claimed to make over $11.00 in profits after paying for gas, food, and photo supplies, good wages for such a life of adventure.[9]

The lure of independence—both financial and personal—was used to attract young people to itinerant photography in the 1910s and 1920s. A 1913 ad for the Mandel Post Card Machine told the reader to "get out of the 'time clock' line and the 'pay-envelope' brigade. Be a one-minute photographer."[10] That same year an ad for the Champion Minute Photo Machine claimed its users could make thirty dollars in the first day. "Be your own boss," with the "easiest, quickest, biggest money-maker known," the Champion's ad read, and successful photographers attested to the camera's money-making ability. It could produce a finished photograph in thirty seconds, two hundred photos an hour.[11] Prices for these cameras started at $7.50, a small investment for a guaranteed goldmine of money and freedom.

Itinerant commercial photography begins in photography's earliest days, decades before modern transportation made extensive travel practical. Horse-drawn ambulatory daguerrian galleries used by itinerant portraitists in the 1840s and 1850s gave way to well-appointed railroad car studios, and finally to trailers pulled by automobiles. Daguerreotypes were replaced by ambrotypes, then by albumen prints from collodion negatives, tintypes, silver gelatin prints, and contemporary instant-print materials. But if the methods and materials used by transient photographers change from one generation to the next, with convenience the primary concern, the motives for choosing this difficult and financially unstable line of work have not. Compare, for example, the following two statements:

> There is something about a Flat-Boat Gallery that savors very much of the romantic. . . . Besides we are entirely independent. If business is good, we can remain, if dull we can leave. . . . When we are not employed we can fish or hunt, as best suits our fancy.[12]

Before I left on the wagon, I was just John Doe in the crowd. That was lonely, being a pawn, moving with the rest of the herd. . . .
You can live a full and happy life without jumping in the mainstream American groove.[13]

Colloquialisms aside, these two statements might have come from the same person, but they were made by two itinerants living over a century apart. The first is by Sam F. Simpson, an itinerant daguerreotypist who traveled along the Mississippi River during the 1850s in his "flat-boat gallery." The second is by John Coffer, a contemporary photographer who began traveling across the United States in 1978 in an eighty-year-old wooden wagon drawn by horses and oxen, recreating his vision of the lifestyle of a nineteenth-century tintypist.

Coffer took his romantic fascination with itinerancy to its extreme, selling his condominium, sports car, and other possessions to buy his wagon, antique photographic equipment, and materials for making the wet-plate collodion negatives he uses in place of modern film.[14] In one respect, Coffer is not at all like the photographers he emulates; itinerants in the nineteenth century strove for comfort and convenience, using the simplest photographic technology available that would suit their purposes, and devising ways of making their work and travel easier. For example, John R. Gorgas, an itinerant who, like Simpson, ran a floating gallery on the Ohio and Mississippi rivers, traveled on a sixty-five-foot-long boat, "well appointed," with a good cook, flute, violin and guitar.[15] Gorgas's river life (and we imagine Simpson's as well) was hardly a spartan existence by nineteenth-century standards, unlike Coffer's contemporary re-creation. Gorgas's and Simpson's parallels today are the itinerants who take advantage of the modern niceties of instant film, strobe flash, and comfortable mobile homes, not Coffer with his self-imposed difficulties. Even so, were it possible to bring together Simpson and Coffer for just one day, probably they would at least agree on this: itinerancy is the most rewarding and least confining way of life, and photography makes that life possible.

Itinerant photography is perhaps the medium's oldest tradition, extending from the early daguerreotypists to modern-day Polaroid-shooting street photographers after the tourist dollar. In 1842 the Swiss daguerreotypist J. B. Isenring purchased what is believed to be the first traveling outfit—a carriage complete with living and sleeping quarters, a studio, and a darkroom area.[16] Isenring traveled throughout southern Germany, upper Austria, and northern Switzerland in his carriage or "Sonnenwagen," taking daguerreotypes of people who, unable to make their way to city studios, could not have bought them otherwise (Fig. 1).

Figure 1:
Portrait of a young man,
seated, ca. 1850.
Anonymous
daguerreotype. (Collection
of the author.) While this
portrait is not attributable
to an itinerant
daguerreotypist, it is a
typical example of studio
portraits by early
photographers, traveling
and otherwise.

At about the same time that Isenring was working in Europe, itinerant daguerreotypists in the United States began traveling to small towns and villages just as the limner and silhouette man had before them.[17] Many of these itinerants were apprenticed to the large city studios, like Southworth and Hawes of Boston, which sent their pupils out to work throughout the rural areas of New England, just as contemporary itinerant studios send their photographers to small town department stores. One of Southworth's students, Sarah Holcomb (perhaps the first woman itinerant photographer), soon discovered some of the difficulties in transporting the necessary supplies through cold New England. On arriving in Claremont, New Hampshire, in 1846, where she was the first operator to arrive there in a year, Holcomb found that all her chemicals were frozen.[18] A bottle of bromide had burst, preventing her from making any daguerreotypes until more could be sent from Boston. Holcomb's story indicates the role of itinerancy as a rite of passage, an ordeal for an apprenticed photographer to overcome before being qualified to work in an established studio, with the people living in rural areas serving as practice models for inexperienced photographers learning their trade. But it also suggests that *itinerant* photography was seen as an acceptable vocation for nineteenth-century women, an intriguing subject that is beyond the scope of this essay.

In June of 1845 and again the following year, an itinerant photographer named R. S. Patterson traveled throughout upstate New York, stopping in Lockport, Canandaigua, and Niagara. Two letters by Patterson survive in the archives of the George Eastman House in Rochester, New York. These letters are candid records of the excitement and troubles experienced by early itinerants.

The first letter was written on Sunday, June 13, 1845, after Patterson had spent a week photographing in Lockport. Patterson's efforts were aided by an insurance agent named Reed. Reed had run out of policies to sell and busied himself by providing Patterson with moral support and new customers. I have retained Patterson's haphazard spelling.

> He is either in my room pronouncing every good one that I take "capital", or he is drumming up coustomes— that is bringing up people to look at my specimens and opprations and then advising them by all means to have one taken as "it will onely take 15 minutes and the price is so very low too—besides you *can never get them taken any better in Albany or New York if so well.*"[19]

Patterson wrote that his rented room was crowded with people waiting to be photographed, some of them from the city's most prestigious families, including two daughters of a local judge. But others less notable also came to be photographed, including five blacks and one young man who asked to be photographed in drag. (Patterson wrote that he "coloured him up to fitts," that is, he hand-colored the daguerreotype, no doubt giving his sitter rosy cheeks and ruby lips.) While in Lockport, Patterson was joined by another itinerant daguerreotypist named Irving. The two of them worked throughout the week, making forty-two portraits. Patterson's half of the profits came to $19.39, but when he deducted his expenses he was left with only $4.00. The following week was no less busy, but Patterson ran into technical problems when preparing his plates, ruining most of the week's efforts. Poor weather also made work more difficult, and making daguerreotypes in a rented room was surely not easy under the best conditions.

> It is now cloudy (at sunset) and rainy. I am afraid it will be a bad day tomorrow for my business (which by the way is much harder than making fanning mills). I get up at 4 o'clock and work generly till 10 at night sometimes without dinner at all and some times without pissing from one night till the next. I have from 5 to 25 in my room most of the time.[20]

By the following year, Patterson and Irving (also referred to in the letters as "Meade") had worked out a system for photographing and pleasing their customers, with Patterson preparing the plates and taking the portraits and Irving developing the plates and finishing them. If the exposures were not quite right, they persuaded the sitter that they were not too light and too dark, but were the current fashion:

> If the shade was dark Meade would tell them that it was just the touch and that they could sell no other kind in Albany now. If the shade was light I would tell them that some preferd the dark but I like a light shade much the best myself.[21]

Both Patterson and Irving had learned to be shrewd businessmen after a year of professional photography. Salesmanship was as important as craft in itinerant work, perhaps even more so than in regular commercial studios. Traveling was expensive and thus necessitated the itinerant's success. But by the time the customers decided they weren't satisfied with their portraits, the photographer would be in the next town. As we will later see, this method of operating was not peculiar to early itinerant daguerreotypists and eventually, decades later, became a source of conflict between transient and stationary commercial photographers.

Some early itinerants, like Sarah Holcomb and R. S. Patterson, rented rooms to serve as their temporary studios; others used wagon-studios similar to Isenring's, constructed especially for portrait work. These ambulatory studios, also known as "Daguerreotype Saloons" or "rotary establishments," could be quickly set up in any vacant lot or town square. In 1846 the New York *Mirror* wrote: "There is a chap travelling Connecticut, who has fitted out a large apparatus, and is going about like a tin peddler, calling at houses and taking pictures here and there, as he can find customers."[22]

By 1852 at least four such "saloons" worked out of Syracuse, New York, alone. A year later, in Lockport, New York, E. R. Graves and Henry Pruden reportedly built a "mammoth Daguerreotype Gallery on wheels" at a cost of $1,200. This large gallery measured twenty-eight feet long, eleven feet wide, and nine feet high. The studio was "tastefully furnished" and came a equipped with a skylight.[23] Such elaborate galleries were the forerunners of the luxurious cars later provided by the railroad companies for their photographers, such as the car used by William Henry Jackson, said to have "rivaled that of a millionaire,"[24] but they were of course the exception, not the rule. Most itinerants lived in less impressive surroundings and had little or no social standing.

As they went about their work, itinerant photographers met with mixed receptions. Early daguerreotypists making their way across the country were usually, although not always, well received. In the late 1840s a young itinerant, James F. Ryder, traveled to rural areas to photograph, seeking not adventure but a solution to personal problems, which Ryder called "a natural diffidence and lack of confidence in myself." He recalled:

The home-coming farmer gave me pleasant greeting. The boy with torn hat and trousers rolled half-way to the knee, as he fetched the cows from pasture, hailed me with "Take my likeness, Mister?" The village lasses, shy and sweet, gave modest bows, as they met the "likeness man." I was regarded with respect and courtesy.[25]

For many people in the nineteenth century, itinerant photographers brought a powerful and deeply desired object to their doorstep that would have otherwise been unobtainable, reserved for the city dweller or those able to travel to city studios. Photography was still only a few years old and marvelous—nearly magical. Some itinerants exploited this aura of mystery surrounding the photographic process, a process that to nonphotographers seemed dramatic, confusing. After posing the sitter and clamping his head in place with a special brace to prevent any movement during the long exposure, the daguerreotypist disappeared to his darkened closet to prepare the plate. He soon returned, exposed the plate, and quickly retreated to his darkroom to develop the image. When he finally emerged, he held the sitter's likeness in his hand, fixed on a mirror-like plate. The image shifted, appearing and disappearing, depending on how it was viewed, and was surely far more wonderful and confounding to those early viewers than it is to our sophisticated eyes.

As Robert Taft wrote in his *Photography and the American Scene*, "like magicians, they readily acquired the title of professor, a title which has always covered a multitude of sins, mostly of omission."[26] Itinerants less honest than James Ryder may have been a small percentage of the profession, but a town that had been "taken" by a "professor" who, offering to teach the art and science of daguerreotyping to local residents, promised a great deal, accepted payment in advance, and then left town in the middle of the night, would naturally view all subsequent itinerants with suspicion.

While the magical aspects of the daguerreotype sometimes allowed for the schemes of con artists, they could also cause great problems for sincere photographers owing to the public's misunderstanding of photography in general. Taft cites a telling incident, merely one of many similar stories.

A young operator, in his traveling van, had reached a small inland town in Madison County, New York, and after advertising his profession he opened the van for business. Among the first of his customers were two respectable young ladies (all the ladies of that day apparently were respectable). The "Professor" posed the first young lady and then retired into his darkened cubby hole to prepare the silver plate. The second young lady took advantage of the operator's absence to satisfy the age-old woman's curiosity by peeking into the camera. Imagine her surprise to find her friend upside down on the focusing glass. "Oh, Katy," she exclaimed, "you are standing on your head." Katy leaped from her chair in great confusion, and both ran with unmaidenly vigor from this den of iniquity that had so grossly insulted their girlish modesty. They were not content with running, however, for they spread the news of their experience to the villagers, with the result that an indignant mob formed, besieged the van, and finally sent it rolling over the hill, where it and its contents were destroyed; the operator felt lucky to get away with his life.[27]

Even without Taft's embellishments, this story indicates the rather precarious position itinerants could and often did find themselves in.

In the 1870s, the itinerant tintypist George Parke ran up against a situation where he felt deception was his only alternative (Fig. 2). Parke had spent a profitable day working from his tent at a fair in west Texas, making simple portraits just as county fair photographers do today. While closing up their makeshift studio for the day, Parke and his assistant were besieged by four "typical cowmen, waving guns and staggeringly drunk."[28] These inebriated Texans refused to leave without having their "pictur tuck."

> Knowing the light was too poor to make a successful exposure, I hastily ran through a pile of the day's rejects and found four that portrayed a quartette group, although all of different persons. My partner made a few deft manipulations of the camera and passed them to the vociferous four, who paid and departed satisfied, too drunk to note the substitutions.[29]

Parke and his partner felt that they had cleverly handled this difficult situation, outwitting the cowboys with substitute pictures. Satisfied, they went to bed. What they didn't count on was the drunk cowboys sobering up before they left town, at least enough to examine their portraits carefully. They did, and Parke and his assistant found themselves "suddenly awakened by a fusillade of shots which passed through the tent, uncomfortably close to our shrinking forms."[30] Narrowly escaping the tent and gunfire tearing through it, they took refuge and watched the cowboys destroy their outfit. Finally, the Texas Rangers arrived to settle the affair. The cowboys paid for the damage to Parke's equipment, minus the cost of the fake tintypes.

Charlatans, incompetents, and suspicious characters were not uncommon on the frontier; on occasion, photographers joined their ranks. In 1886, the *Santa Fe Weekly Reader* published an account about Henry Wimer and his companions—a "quack doctor" and a Mrs. Moore, "who had a notoriety for ambivalent marital affairs."[31] In 1885 the three moved to Watrous, New Mexico, where they rented a house next to a hotel. While the *Reader* did not specify their professions, Mrs. Moore was probably a

Figure 2:
George Parke, itinerant tintypist
(left), *with his two assistants,*
standing in front of Parke's wagon,
ca. 1875. (Courtesy CBS
Magazines.) Parke's portable studio
consisted of a two-wheeled cart with
a "house-like body covered with
oilcloth, a tarred tin tank for a
bottom, a heavy curtain at the rear,
and an orange-fabric window in
front. The fittings were a keg and
spigot for washing water, shelves for
trays, and bottles and a wood-
encased glass-tank for the silver-
bath." A 5x7 wet-plate camera with
one holder and a sturdy tripod
completed his outfit.

prostitute, the doctor an abortionist, and Wimer a purveyor of pornographic photographs. Whatever the case, the three travelers were ordered to leave town by an "indignation meeting" of local citizens, who threatened to tar-and-feather the sinful threesome. The photographer, the doctor, and the woman left on a train for Las Vegas, and no doubt subsequent itinerant photographers hoping to work in Watrous, New Mexico, received less than enthusiastic greetings.

Although by the twentieth century most people understood the mechanics of photography and the fractious and immoral frontier had been tamed somewhat, the mistrust for itinerants that began in the earliest days of the daguerreotype persisted. In fact, it became more active. The high-pressure sales techniques common in the 1920s were of course used in photography and especially by itinerants. Usually they were coupled with an attractive gimmick, such as the "bargain coupon," a device that continues to be used today by department store photographers. In the twenties and thirties, coupon outfits went door to door selling inexpensive, introductory coupons intended to bring in people who otherwise might not go to the trouble and expense of having their portraits made. The coupon buyer received several photographs for a very low price, perhaps as low as twenty-five cents.[32] Of course, the photographers hoped that once the original photos were sold, the customer would want to order more, at full price. Many customers disliked coupon outfits; they resented being tricked into buying more than they originally wanted. Local studios had a hard time competing with the low coupon prices and naturally resented these traveling photographers. In March 1931, *Pittman's Trade Tips* published the following poem written by commercial photographer Dan Hunt:

NOTICE TO THE PUBLIC

Beware of the faker passing through,
Peddling cheap coupons out to you,
Here today and gone tomorrow
Caricatures that cause you sorrow,
The phony schemes of coupon fakers,
Who offer their trash to innocent takers,
Should be made known, so we warn you
Leave coupons alone or you may rue
Your photo to last, made good and true,
Makes an impression on others of you,
Beware of the fakers just passing through
With trashy coupons held out to you.[33]

While Hunt displays little talent as a poet, his point is clear enough: itinerants were lousy photographers and fakers as well. And even if they were competent photographers, their high-pressured sales pitch often drove away customers, as the following account illustrates.

Mr. and Mrs. Dave Berlin ran the Berlin Studio in Corpus Christi in the 1930s, making formal studio portraits and other standard commercial fare. Mrs. Berlin recalled when a coupon crew set up a studio nearby: "All they had was a little place with a background; they would just snap the pictures and everything was mailed out."[34] One day a man who had gone to the coupon studio came to Mrs. Berlin, obviously upset by his experience. He told her he had bought a coupon on the street for this studio and had gone to the trouble of getting his family dressed up and bringing them in to be photographed. The resulting family portrait may or may not have been an acceptable picture, but when the photographer tried to pressure them into buying more photographs than they originally wanted, the father became very angry, throwing the already paid-for picture down and taking his family around the corner to the Berlins' studio. There Mrs. Berlin told him, "We're here all the time. We don't just come in and put up something for awhile and get out . . . you have to treat a person right when you make your home in the place."[35]

Through such accounts, an image of itinerant photographers begins to emerge. The question is whether it is accurate? Surely some itinerants were high-pressure salesmen; others were merely incompetent. Many older studio photographers today remember itinerants as drunkards, and some of them probably were. But many were no more or less than small-time operators without enough capital to set up their own studio, and still others must have simply preferred traveling to remaining in one place. In the 1930s, when the Depression hit the commercial photographer just as it did the tenant farmer, some must have taken to the road out of sheer desperation.

Living on the road in the 1930s was difficult. Modern conveniences were just becoming available to middle-class Americans; most urban families owned a washing machine but not a refrigerator. But to travelers such things were luxuries. Dr. Lorena Jean Tinker, daughter of Corpus Christi photographer Dr. John F. "Doc" McGregor, grew up around her father's studio in the thirties. She recalls the itinerants who occasionally borrowed his facilities:

> They would not be shaved a lot of times and looked pretty ragged. They'd wear just a miserable suit because then men didn't wear sports clothes, if you wanted to have any business at all. They'd wear real seedy looking suits and shirts that didn't look very clean. . . . They didn't look very well groomed, that's my impression. They looked hot and perspiring, really worn down.[36]

If some itinerants looked "worn down" and seedy, we should bear in mind that those were the days before wash-and-wear and the polyester suit. Certainly most of them tried to look professional. When the photographer George Chappell wrote his book *The Itinerant Photographer* in 1936, he noted the two "don'ts" of itinerant work: "don't forget to dress neatly," and "don't forget to be courteous."[37] Paul Holt, the itinerant who wrote the book *$50 a Week with Camera and Car*, advised aspiring itinerants to be direct, cheery, and "good talkers." They should always be pleasant and polite—"never the 'fresh' attitude. People won't stand for this."[38] The itinerant who worked in Corpus Christi must have both appeared respectable and been a good talker. Otherwise he could not have convinced so many different kinds of people to pose for him, people from all social classes and ethnic groups, from lawyers to laborers to women in beauty shops having their hair done to cooks in the local cafes.

So far I have discussed only a few of the many types of itinerant photographers. The first were portraitists who traveled in wagons, by boats and, later, by rail (Fig. 3). Portraiture is the oldest tradition within itinerancy and is still practiced today. Related to this genre is work done by photographers like Monroe and Ellis, who traveled across the upper Midwest photographing families in front of their homes and schoolchildren in front of their schoolhouse (Figs. 4 and 5). Herman Benke, a photographer who traveled through Wisconsin, Illinois, and Kansas, illustrates another type of picture commonly made by itinerants (Figs. 6 and 7). Benke, a bachelor and amateur botanist, made a series of pictures in Manitowac, Wisconsin (where he lived for several years) that typify his work.[39] He photographed people at the workplace, but brought them out into the sun and posed them in front of their business, not within the store as the Corpus Christi itinerant did three decades later.

Other itinerants specialized in different types of pictures, including those made by traveling postcard photographers such as Sherman Gillett. Like Benke, and Monroe and Ellis, Gillett worked in Wisconsin, a state whose traveling photographers are better known than others because of the efforts of Paul Vanderbilt at the State Historical Society of Wisconsin. (Other states undoubtedly had as many itinerants as Wisconsin, but their photographs are not so well preserved.) Gillett traveled primarily in Wisconsin, covering less territory than some but making a set of remarkable views of small midwestern towns, from Ableman to Yuba (Fig. 8). Less common are the photographs by William Roleff who photographed in Minnesota lumber and mining camps in the 1910s (Fig. 9), and by Edgar Linton, a Kansas City photographer who in 1910 began a trip around the world financed by the photographs he made en route (Fig. 10).[40]

Perhaps the most common type of itinerant was the pony photographers, "kidnappers" who relied on the surefire combination of children, ponies, and cowboy outfits (Fig. 11). While most of these photographers worked alone, there were large crews of them in the 1930s: one man in New York had eighteen ponies and photographers working for him. Each morning the teams were taken out to the suburban areas around the city, dropped off to work for the day, and then picked up in the afternoon.[41]

Figure 3: (Opposite, above)
Floating Photo Gallery of J. P. Doremus of Paterson, New Jersey, who covered the Mississippi River from the Falls of St. Anthony to the Gulf of Mexico. Stereograph, no date. (Courtesy the New York Historical Society, New York.)

Figure 4: (Opposite, below)
Camp with three photographers' darkroom wagons, belonging to C. R. Monroe and N. L. Ellis. Black River Falls, Wisconsin vicinity (?), ca. 1893. (Courtesy State Historical Society of Wisconsin, Charles Van Schaick Collection.)

Figure 5: (Above)
Teacher and students posing by schoolhouse, Black River Falls, Wisconsin vicinity, ca. 1895. Attributed to C. R. Monroe or N. L. Ellis. (Courtesy State Historical Society of Wisconsin, Charles Van Schaick Collection.)

Figure 6:
Herman Benke with camera gear,
Manitowoc, Wisconsin, ca. 1915 (?).
(Courtesy State Historical Society of
Wisconsin.)

Figure 7:
Millinery shop, 108 North 8th(?),
Mrs. Theresa Vollendorf, proprietor,
Manitowoc (?), Wisconsin, ca. 1898.
Herman Benke. (Courtesy State
Historical Society of Wisconsin.)

Figure 8:
Eck's Pharmacy, Black Earth, Wisconsin, November 1925. Sherwin Gillett. (Courtesy State Historical Society of Wisconsin.)

Other photographers worked independently, making lifelong careers out of kidnapping, like William Freeman of Dallas, Texas. Freeman, born in 1910, began photographing kids on ponies in the mid-1930s and in 1980 was still working steadily. "There used to be a bunch of us who did this kind of thing," Freeman recalls, "but I think I'm the only one left now. There was another guy but he died a few years ago."[42] At one time, Freeman would photograph forty or fifty children a day: "I'd shoot pictures of kids all day and work in the darkroom at night."[43] Although most of Freeman's work was done in the Dallas area, he also traveled with his ponies to Mississippi, Tennessee, and Kentucky. Today Freeman chooses his neighborhoods at random and works only when the weather is good and he feels like working.[44]

In the 1930s when William Freeman was beginning his career as a kidnapper in Texas and the South, and large kidnapper crews were drumming up business in the New York City area, street photographers worked the sidewalks of Manhattan, photographing not children on ponies but pedestrians on the run. Robert Winkler began his street photography enterprise in Europe, where in the late 1920s he had a crew of six photographers working for him in Germany, Switzerland, and France.[45] In 1929 he brought his business to New York City and by 1935 had twenty-

Figure 9:
Sharpening Saws,
Kileen and Co.,
Hinsdale Camp #1,
Minnesota, 1914.
William Roleff.
(Courtesy Minnesota
Historical Society.)

Figure 10:
City Hall, Panama
City, 1911. Edgar
Linton. (Courtesy
Dale Monaghen,
Kansas City,
Missouri.)

seven outfits working in various parts of the city. Winkler's crews used a modified movie camera, such as the Acme 35mm Street-Snapping Camera, loaded with 100-foot rolls of movie stock film. A light finger on the trigger exposed only one or two frames at a time; the "Candid-Cameraman" could average 1,500 shots per roll.[46] People on the street were often unaware that they'd been photographed until the photographer handed them a coupon listing the negative number, photographer's address, and cost of the prints (Figs. 12, 13, and 14). About 10 percent of all people snapped ordered the twenty-five-cent photos; sales of only 6 percent were necessary for a profit.[47]

During the Depression, street photographers were common sights in most American cities; in fact, Winkler's success sparked a great deal of interest among commercial photographers needing to make some extra money. In May 1935, *The Professional Photographer* published an article about Winkler and his methods, along with a sample coupon for commercial photographers to copy.[48] In August 1936, the *Houston Press* published an article on street photographers in that city titled "Sidewalk Cameramen Snap 70,000 Houstonians—and Keep Snapping."[49] The article included a photograph with the caption "A camera gunner at work on Main Street" showing one of the photographers at work, handing a coupon to an attractively dressed woman as she walked by. According to the article, the street "gunners" had been in Houston since the previous fall and showed no sign of leaving.

Figure 11:
Young girl on pony in frontyard, ca. 1920. Anonymous. (Collection of the author.)

Figure 12:
Street photographer's coupon, front and back, ca. 1920. (Courtesy Richard Pearce-Moses, Austin, Texas.)

Not all street photographers received such positive publicity as those working in Houston. In Manhattan several notices appeared in the *New York Times* in 1936 and 1937 regarding the annoying street cameramen, most often with the authors calling for ordinances to eliminate them. One typical article concerned nine street photographers who were fined two dollars each and ordered to return their cameras to their employers. The magistrate, Anthony Burke, pointed out the dangers of being photographed by them: "You men are pests and nuisances. . . . suppose you took a picture of a married man and some woman not his wife, or a married woman and a man—you might not mean to, but you might get them in trouble."[50]

Potential customers wrote the *Times* as well, their letters to the editor expressing their concern and annoyance:

> The activities of photographers who so grossly impose on the privacy of individuals are an annoyance much resented by many people and certainly serve no useful purpose. They should be removed from the streets.
>
> (signed) John B. Harris[51]

> About a month ago a man with a camera forced into my hand a card bearing the information that my picture had just been taken and I could have it within a few days upon remittance of 25 cents and postage. Being a "sucker," I complied and I am still waiting for the picture. Several of my friends have had similar experiences. I feel that this new racket should be exposed.
>
> (signed) Babs Courtney[52]

Figure 13:
*Couple walking down
street, October 9, 1948.*
Anonymous street
photographer. (Collection
of the author.)

Figure 14:
*Young man walking down
street, ca. 1948.*
Anonymous street
photographer. (Collection
of the author.)

Since no laws were actually broken by the street photographers, New York courts had to imagine some other way to control these photographers who invaded peoples' privacy and stole their money. They found an ingenious solution when they realized that most people threw their coupons on the sidewalk instead of saving them to order prints. This amounted to littering, and the courts held the photographers responsible. In 1937 two street photographers were fined $10 each, and the judge regretted that there was no more serious charge that could be brought against the two "pirate photographers."

> Every citizen has a right to his privacy and should not be
> photographed without his or her consent. If a citizen who resented
> being photographed would swear out a disorderly conduct
> complaint against men like you, I could give you six months.[53]

Not everyone resented being photographed on the street or feared that they might be caught with the "wrong person." Some, like Fred Rose,

Figure 15:
Street photographer's camera and display, Lima, Peru, 1975.
Benjamin Porter.
(Courtesy of the artist.)

were flattered by the attention. "There is some consolation in being pestered by the lads on street corners who take snapshots. It signifies, at least, that one looks prosperous enough to be the owner of two bits and that is something these days."[54]

Today, the camera gunners' equivalents are the Polaroid-shooting photographers seen in tourist areas like Times Square or the Alamo in San Antonio, where for a few dollars one can buy a full-color portrait, sometimes even mounted in a folding mat. The quality of these Polaroids varies widely. I've seen quite beautiful color portraits done by a young street photographer (and ex-art student) in Manhattan's Lower East Side, and really terrible pictures by other street photographers using the same basic materials. Their prices, however, were the same, about $3.00 per photograph. Still other photographers today fall loosely within the definition of "itinerant," such as Sharon Smith, a New York City photographer/artist who earned her living for seven years by photographing people on the beach at Coney Island and, later, Manhattan clubgoers. Smith worked exclusively with an SX-70, selling her pictures for $5.00 each.[55] Because commercial clients were also the subjects for her personal work, she was able to support herself and pursue her own artistic interests simultaneously. More traditional itinerants still work today in Third World countries, such as Guatemala and Peru (Fig. 15). These itinerant photographers use home-made cameras with a self-contained developing system and carry their painted backdrops with them.[56]

In his 1936 book *The Itinerant Photographer,* George Chappell wrote that the true itinerant stayed on the road from spring to fall.[57] In the winter months, he would stock up on supplies, organize his equipment, plan the next trip, and relax. Many itinerants no doubt planned their travels to avoid cold northern regions in the winter while taking advantage of warmer climates. The Corpus Christi itinerant took the pictures in this book in February, when the weather was relatively mild, rather than going there during the hot and humid summer months or spending his winter in the North.

Itinerant portrait photographers often worked in circuits, returning to the same town every few years. Even after 1900, photographers in small, rural towns were in great demand, and their profits could be enormous. In the 1910s, San Antonio photographer E. O. Goldbeck received a letter from his father encouraging him to come work in Alice, Texas, where "two young fellows a year ago made $1,100 in two days."[58] A thousand dollars in two days is an impressive amount of money even by today's standards; in the 1910s, it was a staggering amount.

Around the same time, another young Texas photographer, L. A. Shugart, was starting up an itinerant business. Shugart, who was eighteen at the time, worked a circuit throughout Texas, setting up in a town and remaining there one to three months. After he married and had three children, he continued living on the road, taking the entire family with him wherever he went. They lived in one trailer and worked in another.[59] The children went to hundreds of schools while growing up on the road, although their problems were lessened somewhat by their father repeating a circuit each year. Eventually the family settled in Levelland, a small Panhandle town that lives up to its name, and continued to operate the itinerant studio from there. Shugart's two sons, L. A., Jr., and W. H., joined their father in business for many years, but after World War II, only L. A., Jr., continued working as an itinerant (Fig. 16). In 1952, Shugart Studio photographers began working through department store promotions rather than independently as they had before. This move reduced their operating costs and increased their profits. Today the studio is run by L. A., Jr.'s wife and their son, Woodward. In 1983, seventeen photographers worked for the studio, including three women.

The Levelland office schedules circuits for all their photographers; arrangements are made several weeks in advance. The photographer goes into the store, such as a Gibson's Discount Store, and sets up a temporary studio among the record racks and check-out counters. Each photographer uses the same simple blue backdrop, stand lights, and camera. They bring only a few props, mostly children's toys, and a blue carpeted box to sit on. The photographer takes the portraits and then sends the exposed film back to the main office in Levelland where it is processed and printed. The prints are then sent back to the store. In the meantime, the photographer goes on to the next scheduled town.

Figure 16:
Shugart Studio Trailer, ca. 1955.
(Courtesy Shugart Studio,
Levelland, Texas.)

Figure 17:
Shugart Studio coupon,
front and back, 1983.
(Collection of the author.)

The initial price is ninety-nine cents for nineteen wallet-sized color portraits (Fig. 17). This money is sent to the studio along with the exposed film; the photographer receives a commission out of the ninety-nine cents but no additional salary. All supplies, camera repairs, and advertising are paid for by the studio.[60]

The department store receives no rental fee from the studio; its profit comes from a percentage of selling the 5×7 and 8×10 prints that the studio sends along with the wallet photos. The store also benefits from the increased traffic when people come to be photographed and again when they pick up the finished prints. Shugart's photographers are hired without experience, then trained for thirty days. They generally work six days a week, cover a 300-mile radius, photograph an average of 150 people a day, and make about $34,000 a year.[61] And while they may own a house somewhere within their territory, most of their time is spent on the road. Home is a succession of motel rooms for some, for others a comfortable Winnebago.

Itinerant photographers usually specialized in one type of photography, whether traditional portraits, postcards of residences, or street photography. Photographs from each of these genres can tell us much about certain places and people but very little about the photographers. They tell us only slightly more about the culture influencing them and their subjects. In the portraits, we see evidence of styles of dress and implications of the sitters' social standing. In street photography, fragments of streets and buildings find their way into the background, offering brief glimpses of environment and architecture. But this information quickly becomes repetitive. A hundred pictures of children on ponies, posing outside their homes, tell us little more than just one or two such images.

The Corpus Christi pictures are different. These photographs clearly describe a variety of rooms filled with consumer goods—the physical details of material culture. Even more important, they show the people who owned and worked in those rooms in the context of their professional environment. These photographs are not "documentary"—they were not made with a "serious sociological purpose."[62] Initially, the Corpus Christi pictures functioned as objects exchanged for currency, as a money-generating product for the photographer. Once purchased, they became family mementos pasted into scrapbooks or albums, kept in drawers or boxes along with other family photographs, framed and hung from the walls of the businesses pictured, or even nailed directly to the wall. Later they served as historical records, occasionally appearing in local newspaper articles announcing the remodeling of a store's interior (and nearly always as the "before" picture) or its permanent closing. Now, in this book, they take on the role of historical documents and, to some extent, of art objects.

While the itinerant's pictures were certainly not meant to be viewed as art, we can consider them as cultural artifacts and appreciate the photographer's ability to construct compelling images. To do so does not, I believe, make claims beyond the significance of either the photographer or his pictures.

In February 1934 the Corpus Christi itinerant photographed soda jerk Weldon Cobb as he posed behind the Southend Drugstore's soda fountain (Fig. 18). Here Cobb appears as he would to any new arrival in Corpus Christi. Uniformed and attentive, he is engaged by the photographer and evidently participating in the picture's making. He is not caught in the midst of his work, scooping ice cream or making sodas as documentary photographer Russell Lee photographed another Corpus Christi soda jerk five years later (Fig. 19). Instead, the itinerant chose a method that relies less on timing than candid photography does, first posing Cobb and then photographing him as he looked into the camera. The resulting image, posed yet hurriedly made, seems a cross between a formal studio portrait and a snapshot, a quality found in all the itinerant's Corpus Christi photographs.

Young Lonnie Price worked as a bellhop at Corpus Christi's Plaza Hotel when he was photographed by this itinerant in 1934 (Plate 110). Though Price bought a print from the itinerant ("You look at your gorgeous self and who can resist?" he says today), and kept it along with family snapshots and other personal mementos, he recalls little of how it came to be made. "I remember him taking it, but I don't remember getting it. He was a transient, a photographer off the street who took our picture. . . . I don't remember if he was black, purple or white."[63] Few of his subjects remember the itinerant; he was merely one of many who passed through town for a brief time, leaving behind a few pictures and fewer impressions.

It is impossible to trace this itinerant for many reasons, one being that he did not advertise while in Corpus Christi, although it was fairly inexpensive to take out an ad in the local paper. While this may seem a poor business practice, it does make sense. Our itinerant didn't *need* to advertise his work. He contacted his prospective customers in the most direct and effective way possible—door-to-door solicitation. An ad in the paper would have brought him no additional customers, since he would personally meet each of them anyway as he went about his work. Again, there is no mention of this photographer in the Corpus Christi paper or even in the smaller weekly papers in nearby towns like Refugio, Woodsboro, or Sinton. The photographer's appearance was not a newsworthy item, even in the small towns he passed through. He was certainly not an important arrival to the city; he did not get arrested, and apparently no one complained about his activities. This same itinerant undoubtedly worked in many other towns and cities, and perhaps more glass plates attributable to him will appear in the future. But this seems unlikely; we will probably never know how much work this photographer did over the course of his career, or how long he traveled about the country photographing.

Figure 18:
*Weldon Cobb, soda jerk,
Southend Drugstore, 1101
South Staples, Corpus
Christi, Texas, February
1934.* Anonymous
itinerant photographer.
(Courtesy Harry Ransom
Humanities Research
Center, University of
Texas at Austin;
Photography Collection,
McGregor Archive.)

Figure 19:
*Soda jerker flipping ice
cream into malted milk
shakes, Corpus Christi,
Texas, February 1939.*
Russell Lee. (Courtesy
Library of Congress, neg.
#LCUSF34-32264.)

More surprising than the Corpus Christi itinerant's lack of advertising is the fact that he did not stamp or sign his sold prints with his name. At first this would seem professionally negligent; how could anyone order more prints in the future? They couldn't; the itinerant kept no negatives for making additional prints. But though he probably regretted this, he had no choice. He couldn't be burdened with carrying around five hundred glass-plate negatives, a worthless commodity outside the Corpus Christi area. And if he made five hundred negatives a month, in a very short time he would accumulate an impossibly large and bulky archive. Once he had given people a chance to buy their photograph and made his sales, he abandoned his negatives.

Though we know little about the Corpus Christi itinerant, we know a good deal about the city he worked in. During the Depression, Corpus Christi suffered less than many other cities owing to industrial growth and the discovery of major oil fields at the western city limits in 1930. The following year, nearly fourteen million dollars in building permits were issued. A seven-million-dollar chemical plant, Southern Alkalai Corporation, was announced for the city's outskirts in 1930. This chemical plant required the extension of the port channel and the laying of new railroad tracks and promised many new jobs to local residents. Construction of the plant began in the fall of 1933; its effect on the city was described by Dale Miller in the December 16, 1933, issue of *Texas Weekly* in an article titled "Industrial Progress at Corpus Christi."

> The lethargy of these heavily laden years is being rudely shattered in this South Texas city by the song of rivet and hammer. Girders are hauled high in the air, wheelbarrows dripping wet cement are raced up long gangplanks and smiles from the surging mass of men and machines transform the picture of depression into one of inspiring progress.[64]

In 1934 the plant began production, using salt and oyster shells from the area to produce basic alkalis used in the manufacturing of glass, soap, refined oil, and gasoline.

What really kept the city going through the thirties was the discovery of oil in the Saxet Field, just west of the city limit. The first well, discovered in 1930, was capable of producing commercial quantities of crude oil. More wells were discovered in the same area, and oil men and dealers in oil machinery and tools flocked to town. Between 1935 and 1936, twenty-four oil companies moved to Corpus Christi, not including lease companies and brokers, drilling contractors, speciality companies, or independent geologists.

> The development of oil fields brought in many workers, specialists in their line, who became permanent residents of Corpus Christi.

As they and their families sought residences here, an acute housing shortage resulted. Real estate values skyrocketed and new construction was soon establishing records. A wave of general prosperity spread over the community. Oil supply houses were established. Merchants increased their stocks. Even the farmers' produce commanded a better price.[65]

By 1936 there were 396 oil wells producing 27,541 barrels of oil daily within ten miles of the city limits, and the lobby of the Plaza Hotel became a favorite meeting place for the independent wildcatters.[66]

During the Depression, Corpus Christi's relatively strong economy must have been very attractive for selling an item as inessential as pictures. Add to this the lure of the Gulf Coast's warm climate and it explains why an itinerant would spend several weeks working there. In fact, some evidence suggests that this same itinerant worked in Corpus Christi at least three times during the Depression. Gus Nicols, who owned and operated the Texas Cafe from 1930 to 1939, has three pictures of the cafe's interior. The earliest picture, taken between 1930 and 1933 (Fig. 20), shows the cafe from the entrance, looking in. Gus is second from the right, standing next to the cafe's then-owner, Bill Madias. Note the placement of the camera and how the photographer framed the scene. Compare this picture to the second photograph (Fig. 21), taken in February 1934, the negative of which is in the McGregor Collection. The framing is virtually identical to the earlier picture. In the 1934 picture, Gus occupies the place of greatest importance; he has by this time become the cafe's owner, and his elevated status is reflected in the picture. The final picture was taken between 1936 and 1939 (Fig. 22). Again, the framing is similar to that in the first two pictures, though the camera's viewpoint seems higher. (The light streaks at the top right were probably caused by an exploding flashbulb.) Again, Gus, the cafe's owner, is positioned in a dominant place.

These three images raise an interesting question. Were they all made by the same photographer, working a two- or three-year circuit through south Texas? This interpretation is suggested both by the visual similarities among the photographs and by the identical type of mounting used for the prints: plain grey cardboard of the same size and grade. More important, the pictures appear to be printed on the same type and weight of photographic paper, with the glass plates masked along the edges in the same crude way. Two or three different photographers would be unlikely to frame a scene in the same way, use the same size negative (5 × 7), the same type of wide-angle lens and open flash, make the same type of crudely masked print on the same single weight paper, mount them on the same plain board, and having done so, neglect to sign the prints or mark them in any way.

But, unfortunately, we don't know whether one, two, or three photographers photographed the Texas Cafe between 1930 and 1939. Although

Figure 20:
The Texas Cafe, 1106 Leopard Street, Corpus Christi, Texas, ca. 1932. Anonymous. (Courtesy Gus Nicols, Corpus Christi, Texas.)

he kept the three photographs (just as Lonnie Price kept his), Gus Nicols does not remember anything at all about who made them or how he bought them. Nicols's memories are of the cafe and the people who worked there with him, and of how he came to America from Greece, began working for his uncles in their restaurant, and finally owned his own cafe. These memories and experiences are much more important to him than who might have taken these three pictures.

Whether the itinerant who worked in Corpus Christi in 1934 was a regular or one-time visitor to the city makes little difference. Either way, he was there to make as many pictures and as much money as possible in a short time. He had no need to establish himself in the community or politely appeal to residents for their business; unlike local studio photographers he did not wait for business to come to him. He sought his customers directly and in person. He was as much a salesman as a photographer. Before he could make his photographs and even have a chance to earn a living, he first had to sell himself and convince his prospective clients that they wanted to be photographed.

An itinerant photographer's ability to earn a living depended on his ability to influence his prospective customer, whether by flattery or by more questionable means. The lengths such a photographer might go to are evident in statements made by one-time itinerant photographer Eugene O. Goldbeck of San Antonio.[67] Although Goldbeck is best known for his Cirkut panorama photographs of landscapes and cities around the

Figure 21:
The Texas Cafe, February 1934. Anonymous itinerant photographer. (Courtesy Harry Ransom Humanities Research Center, University of Texas at Austin; Photography Collection, McGregor Archive.)

Figure 22:
The Texas Cafe, ca. 1937. Anonymous. (Courtesy Gus Nicols, Corpus Christi, Texas.)

world, in 1914 he photographed business interiors much like the Corpus Christi itinerant did two decades later. While this type of work was a sideline for him at an early stage of his career, he concentrated briefly on business interiors while on the West Coast, working in San Francisco, Portland, and Seattle.[68]

Goldbeck approached his prospective customers determined to persuade them to be photographed. "Even though they tell you they're not interested . . . they'll finally say, well, go ahead and make the picture."[69] Showing examples of his work and saying "this is the type of picture I make," Goldbeck offered to make his pictures with "no obligation whatever" on the subject's part. If he met with a reluctant response, he might then say that the pictures were for the Chamber of Commerce or a well-known trade journal (of course, they weren't)—"some line of bull and 99% of them will fall for it." The exposure made, Goldbeck would process and proof the pictures. ("I'd work all day and develop at night. I used to make a darkroom in twenty minutes out of any place, just so I had a bathroom. I'd make a darkroom out of it in nothing flat.") Within a day or two, Goldbeck would return to each business with the mounted prints, offering them for sale at 35 cents each or three for a dollar. "Nine out of ten will buy if you get any kind of picture at all," because like Lonnie Price, people like to look at themselves and will pay for the opportunity.

Working alone, Goldbeck could photograph up to thirty businesses a day, and perhaps five or six hundred in a month depending on the size of the city, a phenomenal amount of work for one person. Many itinerants employed assistants as proof passers or darkroom assistants. "They'd just rent a room with a bath in it. That was the headquarters," Goldbeck says.

> I met a fellow in Seattle—I can't think of the guy's name, I think it started with a C. It's been long years ago, 1914. He had a man that did nothing but stay in the house where he rented a room with a bath. It was really a boarding house. And this fellow made all the prints, got out the proofs and the other fellow was out on the street everyday photographing.[70]

For this type of work to be profitable, a photographer needed a certain degree of control over his materials and subjects. Commerical photography in general does not allow for experimentation. An itinerant needed a formula or set of pictorial conventions if he hoped to depend on his pictures for his livelihood. Looking through examples of photographs of business interiors made between 1900 and 1950, certain conventions in this genre are apparent (Figs. 23–33). These photographs suggest two things: (1) the visual formulas used in this genre were well established by 1934 and so were certainly not invented by the Corpus Christi itinerant, and (2) the Corpus Christi itinerant used those formulas particularly well and even, on occasion, pushed beyond the genre's conventions.

Figure 23:
P. H. Doll Store, Las Vegas, New Mexico, ca. 1900. Anonymous. (Courtesy Museum of New Mexico.)

Figure 24:
H. P. Blakkestad, dealer in musical merchandise, 619 First Avenue South, Minneapolis, Minnesota, ca. 1900. Anonymous. (Courtesy Minnesota Historical Society.)

Figure 25:
*Office Interior (possibly
in a creamery), Morrison
County, Minnesota, 1925.*
Anonymous. (Courtesy
Minnesota Historical
Society.)

Figure 26:
*Blacksmith Shop,
Morrison County, 1925.*
Anonymous. (Courtesy
Minnesota Historical
Society.)

Figure 27:
*Bar Interior, Morrison
County, 1925.*
Anonymous. (Courtesy
Minnesota Historical
Society.)

Figure 28:
*Garage Interior, Morrison
County, 1925.*
Anonymous. (Courtesy
Minnesota Historical
Society.)

Figure 29:
Auto repair, pre-1912.
Anonymous. (Courtesy
Oregon Historical Society,
Ashford Collection.)

Figure 30:
Auto Dealer, Canadian,
Texas, ca. 1925.
Anonymous. (Courtesy
Hemphill County Library,
Canadian, Texas.)

Figure 31:
Fuentes' Cafe, New York City, ca. 1941.
Anonymous. (Courtesy Municipal Archives of the City of New York.)

Figure 32:
Flanders' Bar, San Antonio, Texas, ca. 1941.
Anonymous. (Courtesy Mary Persyn, copy from the University of Texas Institute of Texan Cultures at San Antonio.)

Figure 33:
J. E. Moyer Barber Shop,
Bellwood, Nebraska,
1947. Anonymous.
(Courtesy Nebraska State
Historical Society.)

The development of business interior photography as an itinerant genre coincided with technical developments in photographic equipment and materials. To photograph successfully inside, an itinerant needed an adequate, portable light source, like magnesium flashpowder. By 1890, German portrait photographers, such as C. C. Schirm of Berlin, were regularly using magnesium flash in their studios.[71] In England, photographers became aware of such technical advancements through books like Robert Slingsby's *Practical Flashlight Photography* published in 1890. In this book, Slingsby gave instructions for photographing interiors, recommending the use of wide-angle lenses and rapid, dry glass plates.[72] Four years later, the American Edward Wilson made nearly identical suggestions in his *Cyclopaedic Photography.*[73] The practical concept of photographing interiors with wide angle lenses was rapidly accepted by commercial photographers and itinerants and remains the norm today. To photograph a room without its inhabitants, available light was adequate. But to include people in the interior required additional light. Perhaps the earliest photograph of an interior working environment that includes the workers in the image is Timothy O'Sullivan's "Ore Carriers, Virginia City, Nevada," made in the winter of 1867–68 (Fig 34). Here O'Sullivan used magnesium flash ribbons, a forerunner of the magnesium flash powder used by the Corpus Christi itinerant.

Figure 34:
*Ore Carriers, Virginia
City, Nevada, 1867–68,*
detail of stereograph.
Timothy O'Sullivan.
(Courtesy The National
Archives.)

As we have already seen, many photographers chose to avoid the dangers of volatile flashpowder by photographing the owners of a business outdoors in front of their stores. By 1910 it was far more common for business portraits to be made indoors. Improvements in lenses, glass-plate emulsions and flashpowder equipment made photographing indoors safer and more predictable, lessening a photographer's dependance on good light and fair weather.

Wide-angle lenses and flash tend to dramatize a scene, emphasizing some elements, obscuring others. Usually the effect is to heighten the impact of the image, although a flashy and theatrical technique was no more a guarantee for good pictures in the 1930s than it is today. Looking at the Corpus Christi photographs, it becomes apparent that the photographer knew from experience how to construct an interesting image. He knew where to place his camera, how to emphasize objects and people to indicate their importance, how to use the flashpowder most effectively to illuminate his subjects, and how to make the most of the wide-angle lens distortion of space and perspective. Unlike most other itinerants, he was able to make a striking image on a regular basis, not by accident. But what most sets him apart from the numerous other itinerants who worked in this genre is his evident ability to encourage his subjects to participate with him in the picture's making. In some pictures it seems as though he is

Figure 35:
*Corpus Christi City Health
Department, City Hall, Corpus
Christi, Texas, February 1934.*
Anonymous itinerant photographer.
(Courtesy Harry Ransom
Humanities Research Center,
University of Texas at Austin;
Photography Collection, McGregor
Archive.)

sharing a secret with them or enlisting them in a conspiracy. He was not satisfied to make an exposure from a preestablished vantage point, such as the entrance doorway. Instead, he repeatedly sought out the most interesting place to set his tripod and fired his flashpowder at the moment when his subjects responded to him most directly.

Perhaps the best example of this photographer's ability to go beyond the restrictions of his genre is his picture of the Corpus Christi City Health Department (Fig. 35). In this remarkable photograph, an ordinary office becomes a surrealistic setting. The wall on the left is disconnected from a ceiling we assume exists just out of view and is left to stand unsupported. A woman sits glumly at her desk, surrounded by the artifacts of her job and personal life. She looks into the camera's lens, probably at the photographer's direction, not at the two men to her left. The man standing holds an unidentifiable object in his hand, apparently showing it to the man seated next to him. Both men look at the camera as if they share a secret. Yet for all this apparent complicity, these three people do not directly interact with each other; they respond only to the photographer. And in this image he transformed them from ordinary city workers into characters in a play of his contrivance.

Through the itinerant's camera, Corpus Christi's public spaces become stage sets; local citizens become both actors and audience. The surface of the photograph is the fourth wall, the imaginary boundary existing in the proscenium of the stage, the parameters of which—the picture's frame— are respected by the photographer and seldom violated. All action, all people and objects of importance are centered in the frame. The photographer uses shapes, tones, objects, and even words around the picture's periphery to direct our attention to center stage.

The sense of control in the midst of chaos that is so apparent in these pictures is not a result of the itinerant's artistic concerns, although he did evidently enjoy making pictures. He did not intend to make a personal statement through his directorial approach; his photographs were made to be sold, not for exhibition or publication. To see him as an artist-photographer would be an enormous mistake and misrepresentation of his purpose. His reason for directing is as simple as his primary reason for making pictures: to ensure a consistent level of quality, thus improving his chances of making sales. He was a craftsman, not an artist. Though this statement may seem too obvious, with the tendency to treat previously unknown groups of photographs as mysterious revelations of the photographer's subconscious aesthetic understanding—in short, to mystify the pictures and thus remove them from their context—it is a distinction worth making.

Commercial photographers including itinerants, have a specific purpose for their picture-making. Their job is to render their subject clearly, in accordance with acceptable pictorial conventions of their time (i.e., the kind of picture their client desires) based on well-established precedents.

They must be able to photograph a wide variety of subjects, from the routine to the bizarre, and to produce good photographs of them. At times, the combination of subject with the photographer's skilled rendering of it produces that rare image that contains the quintessence of life. What distinguishes work done by an accomplished commercial photographer from that of a photographer like Walker Evans or Berenice Abbott is not so much the quality of individual images. It is the underlying conception behind each image and its place in the photographer's entire body of work. To put it another way, the difference is in the photographer's intention, which in turn influences how the pictures look and what they mean.

Look, for example, at two photographs of barber shops. Walker Evans's 1936 picture (Fig. 36) was taken in Atlanta, Georgia, while he worked for the Farm Security Administration. A richly detailed print made from an 8 × 10 negative, it tells us as much about the photographer's intention and concerns as it does about barber shops in the 1930's. Evans made this picture for his own, private reasons. (Although he worked under Roy Stryker for the F.S.A. and was given guidelines for photographing, his tendency to ignore those guidelines and follow his own "shooting script" is well documented.[74]) Evans did not need to sell this picture back to the barbers; he had no reason to center the image on them or even include them in the picture. It is an image turned in on itself, a private observation whose meaning was aimed at a very specific audience. On the other hand, the second picture (Fig. 37), made by the itinerant in Corpus Christi, is clearly meant to be sold; not surprisingly, it centers on the barbers themselves along with their possessions.

Unlike an independent photographer such as Evans, an itinerant was necessarily concerned with making a daily profit from his work. The best way to insure a profit was to photograph several people at once. While the cost for exposing a picture of one person was the same as that for a large group, the potential sales from the group picture were much greater. When it was not possible to photograph a large group, an itinerant could still maximize his money-making potential by photographing the various departments of each business. For instance, after photographing the store clerks he might then photograph the owner in his office, the truck driver next to the delivery truck, or the people employed in the warehouse. A good example of this approach is in the McGregor Collection's large number of photographs made at the Nueces County Courthouse, located in downtown Corpus Christi (Plates 84–93). The courthouse pictures, probably made in a single day or two, show the full range of this itinerant's abilities. Here are large group portraits, individuals at their desks, and other groups of various sizes. He was able to convince nearly everyone, it seems, to have their pictures made, from the county judge and sheriff to county clerks, surveyors, and secretaries.

Although we have no biographical or personal information on this itinerant, something can be surmised about his personality from studying the

Figure 36:
*Negro Barber Shop,
Atlanta, Georgia, March
1936.* Walker Evans.
(Courtesy Library of
Congress, negative
LC-USF342-8100a.)

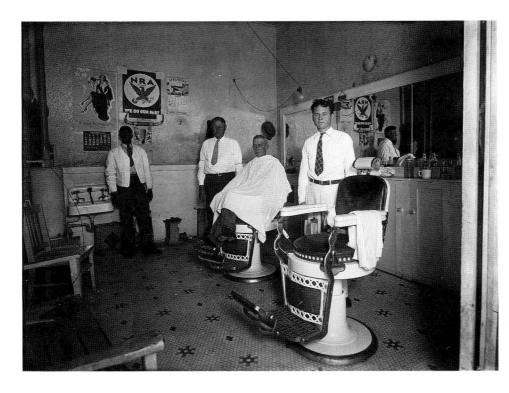

Figure 37:
*Unidentified Barber Shop,
Corpus Christi, Texas,
February 1934.*
Anonymous itinerant
photographer. (Courtesy
Harry Ransom
Humanities Research
Center, University of
Texas at Austin;
Photography Collection,
McGregor Archive.)

photographs. As Walker Evans so aptly stated, "The secret of photography is, the camera takes on the character and the personality of the handler."[75] Or as Berenice Abbott wrote in her introduction to *The World of Atget*, "Every step in the process of making a photograph is preceded by a conscious decision which depends on the man in back of the camera and the qualities that go to make up that man."[76] Looking at the work of this unknown photographer it is apparent that he was a virtuoso in his specialty. But beyond that it seems that in spite of the daily concern of earning his room and board, he actually enjoyed making pictures, occasionally photographing a person or group repeatedly in an effort to get an exceptional image.

Several pictures from Corpus Christi bear this out. For example, the itinerant made a series of five photographs in Biel's Self-Service Grocery. One of them, showing the meat counter (Plate 24), stands alone, outside the sequence of the remaining pictures. It is the other four photographs of Biel's that tell us something about the photographer's working methods. (Figs. 38–40, Plate 25). While their original sequence is not known, they are arranged here in an order based on the photographs themselves.

In the first picture, it seems that the itinerant quickly made a photograph of the store interior and some of the employees from the doorway. It is a plain image and not outstanding, but certainly saleable. However, for some reason the itinerant chose to make a second photograph nearly

Figures 38–40:
*Biel's Self-Service Grocery
#1, 416 Starr Street,
Corpus Christi, Texas,
February 1934.*
Anonymous itinerant
photographer. (Courtesy
Harry Ransom
Humanities Research
Center, University of
Texas at Austin;
Photography Collection,
McGregor Archive.)

the same as the first. Here he has moved farther into the store's interior, photographing the same four men as in the first. Notice the small, barely distinguishable figure standing on the store's mezzanine in the background of this photograph. He appears again in the third picture, alone, sitting in his office on the mezzanine. This is Emil Biel, the store's owner. Apparently Biel spoke to the itinerant while he was photographing the store's employees and agreed to have the itinerant come up to his office to make his picture. (Biel suffered from severe arthritis and may have been unable to go downstairs to be photographed with his employees.) Finally, the itinerant made a single picture of J. W. Buster, Biel's meatcutter, standing alone by the front window (Plate 25). It is a striking image, with Buster surrounded by the lovely light coming through the plate glass, accenting his waved hair. This beautiful image was not made for money; the itinerant had already photographed Buster in the first two group shots and had nothing to gain from making this final portrait. Instead, it seems that this image was made simply because the photographer saw something that he wanted to make a picture of, even though this negative was left behind with all the others.

A second example of the itinerant's tendency to make pictures for pleasure is found in the three photographs of Dr. Arthur Padilla and his receptionist (Figs. 41, 42, and 43). In the first picture, Dr. Padilla and his

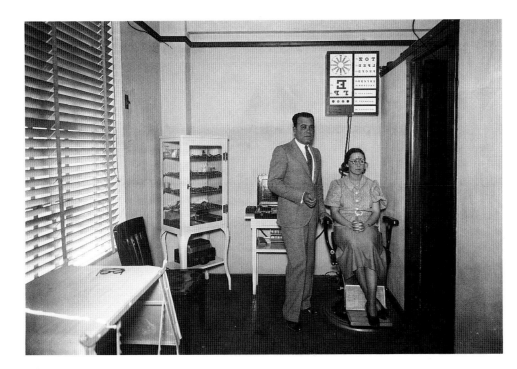

Figures 41–43:
Dr. Arthur Padilla and his receptionist Sarah Kaffie, Corpus Christi, Texas, February 1934. Anonymous itinerant photographer. (Courtesy Harry Ransom Humanities Research Center, University of Texas at Austin; Photography Collection, McGregor Archive.)

receptionist are photographed in the front office. This is the type of picture we might expect from a photographer who walked in off the street, made a fast sales pitch, set up his camera, and exposed a negative. While it is not an extraordinary image, it is saleable. But the itinerant made two additional photographs, one in the examining room. Here Padilla stands next to the receptionist who poses as a patient. His posture is very elegant; she appears somewhat bizarre, wearing special glasses for the examination that is supposed to be taking place. As with the previous portrait of J. W. Buster, no commercial reason is apparent for this second picture; one assumes that the doctor enjoyed being photographed and the itinerant took advantage of a willing subject.

The third photograph, apparently taken on the same day as the second (note the "patient's" dress) was made in a smaller, darkened examining room. Here the doctor has put on his lighted mirror; the "patient" awaits his attention. This image is far removed from the first, both in terms of its formal construction and its psychological and emotional content. It is an image of alienation and separation. The doctor stares out at us with his one visible eye. The receptionist next to him stares at nothing; she gazes blankly ahead as if contemplating something beyond our comprehension. Perhaps she was bored or embarrassed by this extracurricular photographic session; perhaps she anticipated the unpleasant firing of the flashpowder and dreaded the noise and smoke. But no matter how ordinary her thoughts were at that moment, in the photograph her gaze, like the doctor's, seems profound and disturbing. Her nearness to the doctor is only physical; emotionally the distance between them is impassable. In this photograph, the doctor and his receptionist represent the basic solitude of life, a truth that the itinerant, in the process of making a routine picture, was able to communicate.

In the twentieth century itinerants faced a tougher enemy than the hostile and ignorant townspeople encountered by itinerant daguerreotypists—local studio photographers. These photographers began pushing for city ordinances as early as 1915 in an effort to regulate their itinerant competition. The Professional Photographer's Association trade journal, *The Professional Photographer* (originally published as *Abel's Photographic Weekly*), frequently published articles, notices, and correspondence concerning these city ordinances. By the 1930s, their efforts to regulate itinerants increased to the point where they tried not only to restrict their activities, but in some cities to eliminate them and their inexpensive pictures. With the creation of the National Recovery Administration in 1933, studio photographers found an opportunity to control this unwanted—and to them, unfair—competition through federal and state laws along with local ordinances. The state codes could help the studios stay afloat financially by stabilizing wages and prices but only if itinerants and their lower prices were eradicated.

Statistics presented in support of a proposed plan for a federal and state photographic project under the Civil Works Administration (CWA) illuminate the difficulties faced by studio photographers during the Depression.[77] In 1929, the photographic industry employed 55,043 persons; by 1933 this figure dropped to 36,111. According to the plan, of the 250 studios operating in Florida, 150 would go out of business if their landlords demanded payment of back rent. A similar situation existed in Georgia and no doubt in many other states as well.[78]

An additional problem for studio photographers stemmed from new federal and state codes regarding minimum pay rates for interstate commerce. Statistics on Wisconsin photographic studios, published in *The Professional Photographer*, were meant to serve as an example for other states. In Wisconsin cities with populations under 10,000, the minimum wage was set at 50 cents per hour for all studio employees; in cities 50,000 and over, the minimum was 75 cents for photographers, 65 cents for darkroom operators.[79] Studios were required to pay employees at least every few weeks in cash or negotiable check and to pay all expenses for employees required to travel. The State Code Authority of Wisconsin (WRA) further set code prices for sale of negatives and prints, requiring photographers to sell at or above the WRA prices. After November 19, 1934, Wisconsin photographers had to charge at least $3.10 for the first print, $1.50 for the second print, and 22 cents for all additional prints. These prices did not include folders, frames, retouching, or coloring, all of which raised the final price of a photograph considerably.[80] These well-intentioned codes could, in theory, help studio photographers by keeping their prices at a reasonable level, but only if all photographers participated. Of course, the unregulated itinerants did not adopt such price codes. They generally charged $1.00 or less for a 5×7 mounted print, and sidewalk photographers sold their snapshots for as little as three for 25 cents.[81] The price discrepancy created a great problem for Wisconsin studios, unable to compete with the itinerants' low prices without violating the WRA's codes and for studio photographers in states with no price codes, who could not afford to charge so little.

By February 1934 (the month when the itinerant worked in Corpus Christi), *The Professional Photographer* regularly published actual city ordinances designed to "act as an effective weapon against the itinerant photographer."[82] These ordinances were meant to serve as models for studio photographers to follow in promoting similar regulation for their own towns and cities. One such ordinance, sent to the magazine by an unnamed studio photographer in Fort Wayne, Indiana, required new photographic studios to pay a license fee of $200 for the first year of operation and $5.00 per year afterward. Studios in operation at the time this ordinance was passed were exempt from the initial $200 fee.[83] The wording of this ordinance attempted to avoid possible questions of discrimination; itinerants were not singled out, and the ordinance applied to all commercial photographers. However, because this ordinance affected only new studios in Fort Wayne and because $195 of the initial fee was refunded after the first full year of operation, clearly the group most affected by the license requirement were the transients setting up temporary studios for a few weeks or street photographers in town for a few days. Since noncompliance with the ordinance resulted in fines varying from $50 to $100 or possible jail sentences up to six months, itinerants were effectively deterred both from paying the exorbitant licensing fee and from trying to work without one.

In addition to Fort Wayne's licensing ordinance, a general order issued to Fort Wayne police officers instructed them "to pick up all persons found carrying cameras and tripods, and not having license."[84] Two such unlucky photographers working for the Logan Studio of Chicago were arrested and released on $100 bond. The studio's representative went to Fort Wayne to argue the case, but as H. Ross Masterson, president of the Professional Photographers of Fort Wayne, wrote, "After a conference with the city attorney, [the Logan representative] decided to plead guilty and pay the fines for the two men, amounting to $50 plus $55 costs. So I guess the ordinance is ok."[85]

In Waco, Texas, the 1934 city ordinance regarding licensing fees was even more extreme than that in Fort Wayne. Waco required all itinerants to post a $1,000 bond, pay a $10 license fee, and an additional fee of $50 for every solicitor assisting them.[86] For an itinerant who employed an assistant proofpasser, an initial outlay of $1,060 was necessary before the first negative could be exposed; $60 of this was nonrefundable. While ordininaces such as this were clearly discriminatory (some were found to be unconstitutional, like an ordinance in Houston),[87] they did prevent itinerants from working in many cities.

The general public didn't feel about the itinerant as the studio photographers did; people eagerly purchased the less expensive photographs. In Buffalo, New York, two itinerants, Davis and Andreus, conducted business for only four days before being arrested for ordinance violation. In this brief period they took in over $600 in orders "from mothers who vied with one another to get their children's likenesses displayed in the store window."[88] These itinerants were the first arrested under Buffalo's new anti-itinerant ordinance; the city fined them $100 each before ordering them to leave town.

The new ordinances came as a surprise to many itinerants, accustomed to working periodically in a city previously open to all forms of competition. On August 7, 1934, two traveling photographers employed by Blank and Stoller of New York found themselves under arrest in Atlanta for ordinance violation. When asked to produce a license, one of the men reportedly responded: "We have a license? HELL, no. Who in HELL ever heard of paying a license to make pictures? We have been coming here for twelve years and we have never paid any license."[89] They were fined, appealed their case, lost the appeal, and presumably never worked in Atlanta again.

In February 1934, Corpus Christi had no city ordinance governing itinerant photographers.[90] The itinerant must have known this when he came to the city; perhaps he felt he had found an opportunity to work that was disappearing in other cities, or was at the least becoming a more expensive and difficult undertaking. The marked increase in regulations against itinerants no doubt made him all the more aware of his social position as a marginal person and outsider. It is not surprising, then, to find some indication of the itinerant's class consciousness in the photographs he made.[91]

When this itinerant photographed the owner and employees of the Nueces Furniture Store (Plate 44), he arranged them according to their importance within the store. The most dominant figure in the picture is, not surprisingly, the store's owner: Joe Simon. He seems relaxed and confident, allowing himself to be photographed in his vest and shirt sleeves. On the other hand, the store manager, to Simon's right, is dressed in the standard business attire of presportswear America—the three-piece suit. This man stands almost at attention, stiffly posing for his picture, obviously concerned about his appearance and position. He is much less dominant in the picture, partly owing to his smaller physique, but also because the photographer did not choose to emphasize him by his placement. Behind these first two men stand four others. None of them wears a suit or vest; they are dressed, not for the public eye, but according to the requirements of their work: for loading and delivering the furniture sold by the store. They are included in this picture because they too may decide to buy a photograph; however, their relative importance within the social hierarchy of the business is made clear by the photographer's positioning them behind the store's owner and manager.

A similar use of physical placement to indicate social standing is found in the photograph of the Firestone tire dealer (Fig. 44). Here four men, all employees of the shop, are lined up equidistant from the camera. That they are not of the same social status is apparent in their clothing and is further emphasized by the photographer's arrangement and framing. The two men on the left occupy higher social standing; they also occupy the exact center of the frame, while the other two men stand right of center. The man on the far left, wearing a suit and hat, is the store's new general manager; he appears confident, in fact, almost arrogant. (This same man is also found in Fig. 3 in the Afterword.) He is clearly the one in control, something we would sense even without knowing his actual position. To his left, a man wears flannel pants, a white shirt and tie. He probably manages the parts department, as his appearance indicates some public contact but no need to greatly impress the business community. He seems somewhat ill at ease, not nearly so confident in his image as the first man. The third man appears to be the shop manager; he is dressed in a mechanic's uniform but wears a tie, indicating a certain amount of authority

Figure 44:
Firestone Tire Dealer, 824 North Chaparal, Corpus Christi, Texas, February 1934. Anonymous itinerant photographer. (Courtesy Harry Ransom Humanities Research Center, University of Texas at Austin; Photography Collection, McGregor Archive.)

Figure 45:
*Jefferson National Life
Insurance Company,
February 8, 1944.*
(Courtesy Indiana
Historical Society,
Bretzman Collection.)

and public contact. That he prefers to associate himself with the first two men is clear in his stance and position; he stands nearer the two other managers and farther from the fourth man, who is clearly the one who does the shop's manual labor, rarely seeing the public in any significant way. This last man too is dressed in a mechanic's uniform, dirty from his work; in the process of installing and repairing tires, he has wiped dirt and grease on his pants. Holding his hands behind his back, perhaps to hide their filth, he attempts to look his best for the camera. And although he is black, his race seems less a determining factor in his status than the job he performs. Had the itinerant not lined up these four men in this way, their social class would still be apparent in their differing appearances. But their stance and clothing, combined with their physical positioning in the picture, eliminate any question of their relative importance in the social hierarchy of the 1930s.

Because he walked into a business unannounced, without an appointment to photograph a place or its employees, the itinerant made pictures that are more accurate representations of 1930s business environments than photographs taken by hired commercial photographers. Storeowners had little opportunity to clean or rearrange their displays, office workers to clean their desks, or employees to put on clean uniforms or their best

Figure 46:
Hollywood Bar, Madison,
Wisconsin, 1935. Melvin
E. Diemer. (Courtesy
State Historical Society of
Wisconsin.)

clothes. If a person's clothes were soiled from his work, then they appear so in the photograph; if the floors were dirty or the paint peeling, they appear thus in the itinerant's picture. By contrast, when a business hired a commercial photographer to photograph the staff, all uniforms were spotless, all surfaces were shining and often, freshly painted (Figs. 45 and 46). The resulting pictures, when considered as documentary evidence of working life and work environments, are little more than glossy advertisements for the business. In fact, such pictures were generally taken for advertisments, to announce a new location or remodeling of a store, or perhaps to include in an annual report. To regard such images, however interesting or well made, as historically accurate representations is misleading at best. One might as well write an analysis of American cities based only on Chamber of Commerce booster pamphlets.

In the Corpus Christi photographs, we are allowed a special opportunity. Here, momentarily fixed, is a cross section of an American city's stores, offices, and industries, appearing as they would to anyone who came there to do business, in February 1934.

1. These collections include a hand-ful of glass plates at the Hem-phill County Library in Canadian, Texas; over one hun-dred glass plates in the Albu-querque Museum; a large part of the Ashford Collection at the Oregon Historical Society's ar-chive; over one hundred 6½ × 8½ inch plates made in Athens, New York, ca. 1915; and ap-proximately sixty plates made in Morrison County, Minnesota around 1920, in the Minnesota Historical Society's archive. In nearly every museum, archive, and small-town historical collec-tion I viewed throughout the country, there were at least a few images of business interiors similar to the Corpus Christi pictures. The genre was wide-spread and common.

2. *Pittman's Trade Tips*, March 1931, p. 9.

3. Richard Rudisill, *The Mirror Im-age*, p. 130.

4. *Ibid.*

5. *Ibid.*

6. Paul Glenn Holt, *$50 a Week with Camera and Car*, p. 3.

7. William E. Leuchtenburg, *The Perils of Prosperity*, p. 146–148.

8. *Ibid.*, p. 5.

9. *Ibid.*, p. 15.

10. *Photo Advertisements A–Z*, com-piled by George Gilbert, p. 30.

11. *Ibid.*

12. Sam F. Simpson, "Daguerreotyp-ing on the Mississippi," *Photog-raphy and Fine Art Journal* 8, (8); quoted in Richard Rudisill, *The Mirror Image*, p. 138.

13. Patrick Reardon, "History Buff Focuses on America," *The Ari-zona Republic* (Phoenix) Octo-ber 3, 1983.

14. "Roving photo buffs develop sim-ple life with old techniques," *Austin American-Statesman*, December 19, 1983, p. B-13.

15. John R. Gorgas, *St. Louis and Canadian Photographer*, 23 (1899): quoted in Beaumont Newhall, *The Daguerreotype in America*, p. 71.

16. Helmut Gernsheim, *The History of Photography*, p. 161.

17. See Neil Harris's book *The Artist in American Society* for a dis-cussion of itinerant painters in the early nineteenth century, p. 69–72.

18. Beaumont Newhall, *The Daguer-reotype in America*, p. 70.

19. Grant B. Romer, "Letters from an Itinerant Daguerreotypist of Western New York," *Image* 27 (1): 14.

20. *Ibid.*, p. 16.

21. *Ibid.*, p. 17.

22. Beaumont Newhall, "Ambulatory Galleries," *Image* 5 (9): 205.

23. Newhall, *The Daguerreotype in America*, pp. 70–71.

24. Newhall, "Ambulatory Galleries," p. 205.

25. James F. Ryder, *Voigtlander and I in Pursuit of Shadow Catch-ing*, quoted in Rudisill, *The Mirror Image*, p. 136.

26. Robert Taft, *Photography and the American Scene*, p. 48.

27. *Ibid.*, pp. 65–66.

28. George Parke, "The Tintype Pho-tographer of the Seventies,"

Photo-Era 63, no. 4 (April 1929): 194–95.

29. *Ibid.*

30. *Ibid.*

31. Richard Rudisill, *Photographers of the New Mexico Territory 1854–1912*, p. 62.

32. Dr. Lorena Jean Tinker, taped interview with author, Corpus Christi, Texas, June 1982.

33. *Pittman's Trade Tips* (March 1931): 2.

34. Mrs. Dave Berlin, taped interview with author, Corpus Christi, Texas, June 1982.

35. *Ibid.*

36. Dr. Lorena Jean Tinker, interview.

37. George Chappell, *The Itinerant Photographer*, p. 25.

38. Holt, p. 56.

39. Roland G. Fischer, "H. C. Benke: A Profile; H. C. B. as I Knew Him," typed manuscript, State Historical Society of Wisconsin, Iconographic Collection.

40. Edgar Linton, "How I Worked My Way Around the World," *Kansas City Star*, May 26, 1912. Typed manuscript of article, collection of Dale Monaghen.

41. Chappell, p. 23.

42. Maggie Kennedy, "A Little Sugar and a Camera and Kids' Dreams Come Alive," *Dallas Times Herald*, December 31, 1980, Section D, pp. 1 and 8.

43. *Ibid.*

44. *Ibid.*

45. "Sidewalk Pictures," *The Professional Photographer*, May 20, 1935, p. 160–61.

46. *Ibid.*

47. *Ibid.*

48. *Ibid.*

49. "Sidewalk Cameramen Snap 70,000—and Keep Snapping," *The Houston Press*, August 26, 1936.

50. "Street Camera Men Fined," *The New York Times*, February 28, 1936, p. 22.

51. "Itinerant Photographers," *The New York Times*, August 27, 1936, p. 20.

52. "Wandering Photographers," *The New York Times*, September 3, 1935, p. 20.

53. "Two Camera Men Fined," *The New York Times*, June 4, 1937, p. 27.

54. "Complimentary," *The New York Times*, August 23, 1935, p. 14.

55. Sharon Smith, conversations with the author, 1985.

56. For a detailed and fascinating description in words and photographs of contemporary itinerant photographers working in Guatemala, see Ann Parker and Evon Neal, *Los Ambulantes* (Cambridge, Mass.: MIT Press, 1982).

57. Chappell, p. 23.

58. Marguerite Davenport, *The Unpretentious Pose*, p. 29.

59. W. H. Shugart, telephone interview with author, Fall 1983.

60. Mrs. L. A. Shugart, Jr., interview with author, Levelland, Texas, March 1983.

61. Carolyn Williams Ramirez (Shugart Studio photographer), taped interview with author, Austin, Texas, April 1983.

62. In his article "Documentary Approach to Photography" (*Parnassus* 10, no. 3 [March 1938]: 5), Beaumont Newhall offers this definition of "documentary."

63. Lonnie Price, taped interview with author, Corpus Christi, Texas, June 1982.

64. Dale Miller, "Industrial Progress

at Corpus Christi," *The Texas Weekly* (Dallas) December 16, 1933, p. 8.

65. *Corpus Christi: A Guide*, p. 188.

66. "Special Oil Edition" *Corpus Christi Caller-Times*, October 29, 1936.

67. See Marguerite Davenport's excellent book on Goldbeck, *The Unpretentious Pose*.

68. Eugene O. Goldbeck, taped interview with author, San Antonio, Texas, October 1982.

69. *Ibid.*

70. *Ibid.*

71. Robert Slingsby, *Practical Flashlight Photography*, pp. 4–12.

72. *Ibid.*

73. Edward L. Wilson, *Cyclopaedic Photography*, p. 463. Previous books on photography published by Wilson in the 1880s make no mention of methods for photographing interiors with wide-angle lenses and flashpowder.

74. For example, see F. Jack Hurley, *Portrait of a Decade*, pp. 60–64, and William Stott, "Documentary Expression Revisited," *Exposure* 24 (1): 9.

75. Leslie Katz, "Interview with Walker Evans," *Art In America* (March–April 1971); reprinted in *Photography in Print*, edited by Vicki Goldberg, pp. 359–69.

76. Berenice Abbott, *The World of Atget*, introduction, n.p.

77. *The Professional Photographer* (February 5, 1934): 86.

78. *Ibid.*

79. *Ibid.* (December 30, 1934): 321.

80. *Ibid.*

81. "Sidewalk Pictures," *The Professional Photographer* (May 20, 1935): 160–61.

82. *The Professional Photographer*, (February 5, 1934): 86.

83. *Ibid.*

84. *Ibid.* (March 20, 1934): 173.

85. *Ibid.*

86. *Ibid.* (July 5, 1934): 18.

87. "Sidewalk Cameramen . . . ," *The Houston Press*, August 26, 1936.

88. *The Professional Photographer*, (July 5, 1934): 6–7.

89. *Ibid.* (October 5, 1934): 177–78.

90. There is some evidence to suggest that an ordinance was passed in 1935, although no records exist as to the wording of this ordinance, why the city decided to enact one, if it was enforced or for how long.

91. I am indebted to Bill Stott for his insight into the relationship between the itinerant's pictures and the class structure of the time.

Plates

All photographs reproduced here were taken in Corpus Christi, Texas, in February 1934 unless stated otherwise, and are reproduced courtesy of the Photography Collection, Harry Ransom Humanities Research Center, University of Texas at Austin. They were donated to the Collection by Dr. John F. "Doc" McGregor of Corpus Christi, Texas.

Addresses are based on the 1934–35 Corpus Christi City Directory.

Plate 1:
Legion Club, 316 Starr Street. Identified people include Luther Reed, bartender. There were five pool tables. A sign on the wall reads: "Do not sit on tables; use the bridges." There are two American flags and a whisk broom on the post.

Plate 2:
Unidentified Bar. Note the Punget gaming device (a type of marble game) on the counter. This game appears in many of the photographs, along with nickel slot machines and early pinball machines.

Plate 3:
Unidentified Bar. The
nickel slot machine on the
left reads "this takes
jackpot and 20."

Plate 4:
Unidentified Bar. The
fourth man back is
Jerome Jalufka from
Violet, Texas. There is a
bowl of boiled eggs on the
bar and a twin marble
table in the foreground.
(This was a mechanical
pinball machine.)

Plate 5:
The Wonder Bar, 307 Peoples Street.
John C. Brooks and Raymond
Uehlinger were the owners.

Plate 6:
Unidentified Cafe. There is a "New Deal" slot machine on the counter. The menu on the wall includes a Dutch lunch with beer for twenty cents.

Plate 7:
Unidentified Cafe. This cafe was probably in the port area, near the main business district.

Plate 8:
Unidentified Cafe, Corpus Christi vicinity. The man seated at the counter is rolling a cigarette. Note the haphazard electrical wiring.

Plate 9:
The Manhattan Cafe, 305 Peoples Street. At right is George Plomarity, the cafe's owner. The city had a substantial Greek population, many of whom operated the better cafes and restaurants.

Plate 10:
The Pier Cafe, corner of Water and Peoples Street on Pleasure Pier. Pictured here in John Govatos, Sr., the cafe's owner. One of the attractions of this cafe were the windows overlooking the bay. Note the Razzle Dazzle gaming device on the counter next to the cash register and the empty Coke bottle in the lower right corner. One can easily imagine the photographer, thirsty and perhaps tired, finishing off a cold Coke as he talked with Govatos and set up his camera. Govatos was a well-known and liked figure in Corpus Christi and friend of Lyndon Baines Johnson. In the 1930s, when Johnson lived in Corpus Christi, he often ate at the Pier Cafe. Govatos is remembered as providing many free meals for hungry men, including LBJ, during the Depression, even though the cafe was one of the finest restaurants in the city.

Plate 11:
Faust Cafe kitchen, Medical Professional Building, 416 North Chaparral Street. This cafe used the Martin System Laundry.

Plate 12:
Grigg's Pig Stand, 2500 Leopard Street. This photograph is one of the few exterior pictures made by this itinerant photographer while in Corpus Christi. It was located at the far end of Leopard Street, away from the central business district. Note the stand's special on hamburgers—ten cents—and the time—3:35 P.M.

Plate 13:
Muttera's Federal Bakery, 613 Chaparral Street. Fred Muttera owned this bakery. This photograph shows the kitchen.

Plate 14:
Muttera's Federal Bakery, 613 Chaparral Street. This is Muttera's sales counter. They sold sliced rye for 7 cents a loaf, a two-layer chocolate cake for 25 cents, a three-layer cake for 36 cents, doughnuts for 20 cents a dozen, and five-pound fruitcakes for $2.00. Pictured on the left is Audry Black.

Plate 15:
Olympia Confectionary, 602 Chaparral in the corner of the Nueces Hotel. Pictured at center is V. K. Hrissikopoulos, who owned the Olympia along with his nephew Charlie. There are exposed cooling coils inside the candy counter to help keep the candy fresh in the warm and humid south Texas climate. The hard candy is kept in jars on shelves on the rear wall. The Olympia was a popular gathering place for Corpus Christi teenagers, who would stop at the confectionary after the movies for ice cream.

Plate 16:
Unidentified Drugstore. The wicker
stools at the soda fountain swung
out when unoccupied.

Plate 17:
Heap O' Cream #1, located on
North Beach.

Plate 18:
Unidentified Grocery. This was not a self-service store. The man behind the counter would fill the customer's order. This store sold Nueces coffee (from a local wholesaler, see Plate 34), Post Toasties corn flakes, Lily White flour, and Spanish salt.

Plate 19:
Unidentified Grocery. This store sold Palmolive soap for 5 cents, National Oats for 5 cents, Nestle's coffee, Hershey's cocoa, Campbell's soup, 50-lb. burlap bags of sugar, Ditlinger's hen scratch, Red Ranger cigars at 2/5 cents, Union tobacco, and Prophet pens or pencils. Note the well-used counter and the neatly stacked canned goods resembling pyramids.

Plate 20:
*Unidentified Grocery, Corpus
Christi vicinity.* This very small
grocery may have been in a small
town near Corpus Christi. Note the
Mexican figurine, which also appears
in the photograph of the Manhattan
Cafe (Plate 9).

Plate 21:
Bonham Brothers' Grocery, 1019 South Staples. Pictured at left is Otha Bonham.

Plate 22:
Unidentified Grocery. This store is
possibly the Alamo Grocery located
on 213 South Staples Street and
owned by Albert Reymond and
Louis Mareck. Pictured here are
"Raymond" (left) and "Albert"
(right), as indicated by the writing
on their jackets.

Plate 23:
Piggly-Wiggly Grocery Store #1, 613 North Mesquite. This photograph shows the store's meat counter. They sold Grade A veal for 19 cents a lb., porkchops for 8 cents a lb., and roast for 25 cents a lb. They also sold Red Heart dog food, Wriggley's gum, Lucky Strikes, and Chesterfield cigarettes.

Plate 24:
Biel's Self-Service Grocery #1 (meat counter), 416 Starr Street. Pictured are Ray Peterson (center) and Joe Peterson (right). Note the N.R.A. sign, which appears in many of the photographs. On the right is a decorative wall fan.

Plate 25: (Above)
Biel's Self-Service Grocery #1, 416
Starr Street. Pictured here is J. W.
Buster, meatcutter.

Plate 26: (Above)
*C. E. Coleman Produce Company,
Agnes Street and Port Avenue.*
Pictured at right is Charles
Coleman, Jr. Note the Western
Union telegraph terminals, Mr.
Coleman's rolltop desk, and his
informal filing system. The woman
has a marcelle hairstyle.

Plate 27: (Opposite, above)
*C. E. Coleman Produce Company,
Agnes Street and Port Avenue.* This
picture was made in the warehouse
and is an example of the itinerant's
ability to maximize his profit.
Pictured in this photograph are over
a dozen men, each a potential buyer,
although we don't know how many
actually bought prints from the

photographer. Shown here fourth
from the right is Johnny Walker,
surrounded by the farm workers.
The vegetable in the foreground is
cabbage, a major cash crop in the
south Texas region.

Plate 28: (Opposite, below)
*C. E. Coleman Produce Company,
Agnes Street and Port Avenue.* One
of the few exteriors in this
collection, this picture was made on
the loading dock. Pictured third
from the right is Ted Vickers from
nearby Sinton, Texas. These three
pictures from the Coleman Produce
Company are examples of the
itinerant's method of photographing
the various departments of a single
business.

Plate 29:
Unidentified Wholesale Grocer. On
the lower left is an ad for I.G.A.
Promotional material on the window
ledge advertised a Gold Medal
giveaway program.

Plate 30:
Unidentified Wholesale Grocer. This is the room visible in the previous plate. To make this image, the itinerant told the woman to sit at the rear desk (where the man had been seated previously), and the man to stand near the left desk. He also pulled down the window shade (to avoid excessive halation) and turned off the bare light bulb. The resulting picture is one of the most remarkable views in the collection.

Plate 31:
Southwest Texas Old Union Beer Distributor, 120 North Mesquite. This business was owned by Lawrence L. Woodman and Browne F. Beasley. Pictured here is Roy Wilder, bookkeeper (left), and a long-haul truck driver on the Corpus Christi–San Antonio route.

Plate 32:
Hausler-Kilian Cigar Company, 1109 Leopard Street.

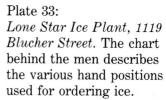

Plate 33:
Lone Star Ice Plant, 1119 Blucher Street. The chart behind the men describes the various hand positions used for ordering ice.

Plate 34:
Nueces Coffee Company, 707 Lester Street. Bins of coffee hung from the ceiling.

Plate 35: (Above)
Unidentified Dry Goods Store. This store sold Stetson hats, shirts for 95 cents, shoes, neckties, and men's pants. The work clothes department was "up-stares."

Plate 36: (Opposite, above)
Unidentified Ladies' Clothing Store.

Plate 37: (Opposite, below)
Abe Klein Clothing Store, 604 North Chaparral Street. An advertisement for Wilson's buffer hose reads: "In the daily grind of heel and toe."

Plate 38:
Lichtenstein's Department Store (men's shoe department), 501–4 North Chaparral Street. Lichtenstein's was the city's largest department store. Note the sign: "Simplex flexies/natural arch/built the doctors' way."

Plate 39:
Loving Clothing Store, 618 North Chaparral Street. They sold shirts for $1.25, Manhattan shirts, dress hats, caps and shoes. Note the spats on the lower shelf of the showcase on the right.

Plate 40:
Unidentified Shoe Store.
A poster in the foreground advertised a lecture and recital by dancer Ruth St. Denis. There was an upstairs office. The upside down boxes on the shelves indicate that those are empty; this was done to keep the shelves from looking empty.

Plate 41:
Richardson's Shoe Store, 703 North Chaparral Street. Pictured here is Mr. Clayton M. Richardson with a customer. The showcase contains womens' shoes, cosmetics, an electric mixer, and a clock. Scarves are on top of the case. There is an advertisement for Buster Brown shoes. Note the open gas heater with the hose running through the shelf of shoes.

Plate 42:
Grossman Brothers Department Store, 1102–4 Leopard Street. Pictured here is Simon Grossman, owner, at right. Grossman's occupied nearly an entire block with different sections for different qualities of clothing. This section sold mens' shirts for 49 cents, socks for 12 cents, and mens' trousers for 89 cents. Note that some of the signs are in Spanish.

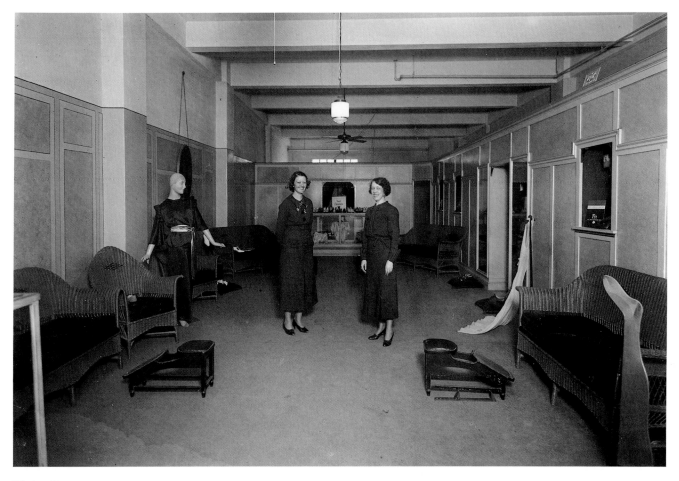

Plate 43:
Cardinal Booterie, 617 Leopard Street. The woman on the right was Mrs. Ernest (Margaret) Cardinal. Note the wicker furniture and shoe clerks' stools. No shoes were displayed in this shop, an indication of its high-class clientele.

Plate 44: (Above)
Nueces Furniture Store, 317 North Chaparral Street. Pictured at right is Joe Simon, the store's owner. Simon was a prominent Corpus Christi citizen. While serving as city councilman, he was responsible for installing the city's parking meters. But he is best remembered for the annual Christmas parties he gave in honor of the city's newsboys.

Plate 45: (Opposite, above)
Allen Furniture Store, 418 North Chaparral Street. Pictured here, from left to right: F. C. Duck (repair and refinishing), George Gabert (floorcovering and drapery installation), unidentified shop helper, Philip Black (salesman and manager of drapery department, W. H. Taylor (manager of repair shop), unidentified salesman.

Plate 46: (Opposite, below)
Unidentified Used Furniture Store. On display are a cast iron cook stove, gas hot plates, sheet iron heaters, a steamer trunk, baby cribs, a bookcase with books, an angel-food cake pan, wooden iceboxes, and a wall hat rack with porcelain tips.

Plate 47: (Opposite, above)
Nueces Hardware and Implement Company, 323 North Chaparral Street. Pictured here on the left is Millard Boyd. Note the footballs suspended from the ceiling with a basketball in the center and the model sailing ship, "The Margaret," which was built by Captain Andy Anderson.

Plate 48: (Opposite, below)
Corpus Christi Hardware (traffic department), 99 South Broadway.

This was the wholesale department of Nueces Hardware. Pictured here is Victor Sohin (seated). Standing from left to right: Wayne "Skeeter" Phillips, J. Harvey Johnson, Boyd Johnson, Alfred Campbell's brother, Lee Hager, unidentified.

Plate 49: (Above)
Corpus Christi Hardware (auto parts department), 99 South Broadway. Pictured from left: Mr. Kirk, Harold Cobb, Jack Kennedy, unidentified.

Plate 50:
W. G. Eubanks Music Store, 305 North Mesquite Street.

Plate 51:
Mireur Leather Goods, 409 North Mesquite Street. Pictured here is Louis Marion (left), Neils Anderson (center), and Joe Mireur (right). Mireur sold leather and canvas horse collars, belts, hand quirts, long hand whips, overalls, and work trousers. Note the Federal Petroleum calendar to the right of Mr. Marion; this same calendar appears in several pictures.

Plate 52:
J. O. Pinkerton, tile contractor, 505 Starr Street. Note the makeshift arrangement for the tile display and the mock fireplace used for tiling demonstrations.

Plate 53:
Roddy Milling Company, Tex-Mex Tracks. Pictured here is J. T. King, bookkeeper. (Mr. King, when shown this photograph in 1982, stated that he had never seen the picture and had no recollection of its being made.) This company sold seed, grain, and Case farm implements. There are advertisements for Dr. LeGear's prescriptions, a common sideline product for feed stores.

Plate 54:
Jack Bonner Printing Company, 415 Peoples Street. Pictured in the center is "Tugg" Tompkins. Two of the five visible presses are a handfed letterpress (center) and a linotype (rear). In the foreground is a perforator; in the rear are California job cases for holding type.

Plate 55:
Plaza Hotel Newsstand, corner of Upper Broadway and Leopard Street. This newsstand sold the Houston Post and Chronicle newspapers and a variety of magazines: *Delineator, True Romance, True Story, True Confessions, Real America, Cosmopolitan, Movie, McCall's, Romance, Silver Screen, Ladies' Home Journal,* and the *Saturday Evening Post.* They also sold an assortment of cigars.

Plate 56:
Shelton-Bailey Ford Motor Company, Refugio, Texas. Pictured at left is Vivian Bailey, owner. This company sold Fords (there is a picture of Henry Ford on the wall behind Mr. Bailey) as well as Firestone tires and tubes. Note the cradle phone on the desk and the hand-crank phone with a switching device on the wall. This was a transition period from hand-crank wall phones and upright desk phones to cradle models.

Plate 57:
Waters Auto Top and Paint Shop, 411 North Waters Street. Lester Waters owned this shop. The men are painting a David Peel ambulance.

Plate 58:
*Roy Murray Ford Dealer,
220-24 North Chaparral
Street.* Note the sign
"Radio is here/$44.50
installed." Radios were
not standard equipment;
they were bought as
accessories and attached
to the dashboard.

Plate 59:
*Unidentified Auto Repair,
Corpus Christi vicinity.*

Plate 60:
C. E. Russell Parts and Machinery,
308 North Chaparral Street.
Russell's sold Perfect Circle piston
rings, Raybestos radiator hoses and
fanbelts, Gould batteries, ball
bearings, spark plugs, and
automobile drive shafts.

Plate 61:
Unidentified Auto Repair, possibly in Robstown, Texas. This business sold new and used tires, fanbelts, battery cables, Champion spark plugs, and Lee's polish. There is a cuspidor on the floor behind the children.

Plate 62:
Goodyear Service Inc., 322 North Water Street. There is a Goodyear poster, a tire safety poster, a truck tire failure poster, and a tire ashtray on the counter. Frederick Nanes was the manager.

Plate 63:
Zip's Battery, 318 North Mesquite Street. Pictured on the right is Cipriano "Zip" Gonzales, the shop's owner. The batteries on the table are glass-jar deep charge batteries.

Plate 64:
Humble Oil Service Station. F. F. English operated this station. They sold Velvet Motor Oil and #997 Motor Oil. Humble gasoline sold for 14½ cents and 19½ cents a gallon. Esso gasoline sold for 16½ cents and 21½ cents a gallon. Note the post for the air and water tubes with the dial for air pressure.

Plate 65:
Jones Texaco Service Station, 1661 South Staples Street. Before Thomas B. Jones bought this station, it was run by Everett L. Powell. They sold Texaco and Indian gasolines and Texaco motor oil.

Plate 66:
Cities Service Oil Company, 1519 Tiger Street. Pictured here is Mr. Neuman. Note the manual gas pump. The area at the top was clear so that the customer could see that gasoline was actually being pumped. There is a lube oil barrel on the right with a pump lying across the top. By this method, oil was pumped into the quart pitcher and poured from the pitcher into the engine.

Plate 67:
Unidentified Oil Field Supply Company. They sold C. S. enamel and Mazda lamps. Note the wooden shelves and bins for storage and the wooden bookkeeper's stool.

Plate 68:
*Corpus Christi Cotton
Exchange, 416–17 Nixon
Building, corner of
Leopard Street and Upper
Broadway, and across
from the Plaza Hotel.*

Plate 69:
*Aransas Cotton
Compress, near the port.*

Plate 70: (Opposite, above)
Texas Motor Sales, 715 North Mesquite Street. Pictured on the left is Joe Early, who later ran his own machine shop. On the left is a line shaft and belt, which indicates that this shop was powered by a gasoline engine. Power tools were hooked up to belts, which were powered by a line shaft that ran along the ceiling. On the right against the wall is a drill press. Lathes are on the left and right.

Plate 71: (Opposite, below)
Boehmer Blacksmith Shop, 405 Laguna Street. Pictured is John Boehmer, owner, on the left. This shop was powered by a centralized gasoline engine. Power tools were hooked up to belts, which were powered by a line shaft that ran along the ceiling. Note the plow shares, the drill press, the power-driven hacksaw, the anvil, and the barrel of water used for quincing. The dirt floor was characteristic of all blacksmith shops.

Plate 72: (Above)
Unidentified Iron Works. The machine on the right is an air hammer.

Plate 73: (Opposite, above)
*Crocker Transfer and Storage
Company, 1019 North Broadway*
(across from the passenger train
depot). This company was owned by
C. M. and J. W. Crocker and is still
in business in Corpus Christi.

Plate 74: (Opposite, below)
*Nueces Bus Company, 1317 Garilan
Street.* There is a three-drawer
wooden filing cabinet, a walk-in safe,
and a map of Texas on the right. The
company was owned by E. C. and
R. E. Ekstrom.

Plate 75: (Above)
*Tex-Mex Railroad Office, Tex-Mex
Tracks, Staples and Kinney streets.*
The man seated on the left is Mr. F.
W. Wright. Note the telegraph
sounder on the desk.

Plate 76:
*Union Central Life
Insurance, #515 Sherman
Building, 317 Peoples
Street.* Pictured here is
Thelma Hatchett,
secretary.

Plate 77:
Unidentified Office.

Plate 78:
Unidentified Office.

Plate 79:
Unidentified Office. On the right is possibly F. B. Cochran, manager of the Anderson-Clayton Company.

Plate 80:
*Harrell Electric
Company, 410 Taylor
Street.* Pictured here is
Harry "Red" Harrell,
owner.

Plate 81:
*W. M. Neyland Realty
Company, 509 Starr
Street.* On the left are
photographs of buildings
and a group of keys to the
buildings that were for
sale. There is a Carl
Haltom ad on the clock
and a Western Union
terminal near the public
stenographer's desk. There
is a window between the
front and back offices; Mr.
Neyland is seated in the
rear office.

Plate 82:
Russell Savage, Attorney, #210 Guggenheim-Cohn Building, 416 Schatzell Street. Pictured here are Russell Savage (right) and Francis Gollihar (Fish), his secretary.

Plate 83:
Unidentified Office, possibly in the county courthouse.

Plate 84:
Office of County Judge Joe Browning, Old 1919 Nueces County Courthouse, Chaparral Street. From left to right are: County Commissioner Frank Allen (from CalAllen, Texas), County Attorney Linton Savage, County Judge Joe Browning.

Plate 85:
Office of County Assessor-Collector Ann Currington, Old 1919 Nueces County Courthouse, Chaparral Street. Miss Currington is also pictured in Plate 89.

Plate 86:
Constable's Office, Old 1919 Nueces County Courthouse, Chaparral Street. Standing from left to right: possibly U.S. Deputy Marshall Dewy Tom, unidentified, "Dugie" Ware (a deputy from Bluntzer, Texas), and L. B. Peckenpaugh. Seated is Constable Bill Eliff.

Plate 87:
Sheriff's Office, Old 1919 Nueces County Courthouse, Chaparral Street. Identified in this picture are: Lloyd Magee (second from left) and Jack Hamilton (second from right).

Plate 88:
Office of County Surveyor Conrad Von Blucher, Old 1919 Nueces County Courthouse, Chaparral Street. On the left is county surveyor Conrad Von Blucher; on the right is N. F. Phillips, from Sinton, Texas.

Plate 89:
County Tax Department, Old 1919 Nueces County Courthouse, Chaparral Street. In the center is Ray Kring, surrounded by (from left): unidentified, unidentified, Miss Palek, Kate Tom, Irene Byfield, Georgia Nold, Ann Currington. Currington is also pictured in Plate 85.

117

Plate 90:
County Tax Billing Department, Old 1919 Nueces County Courthouse, Chaparral Street. The man seated is Beverly Estes; the man standing is Marcus Russell, a salesman for Bowen's printshop. The courthouse was the only building in Corpus Christi with stacked radiators on the ceiling.

Plate 91:
Sheriff's Office (outer), Old 1919 Nueces County Courthouse, Chaparral Street.

Plate 92:
Entrance to Holding Cell of the County Jail, Old 1919 Nueces County Courthouse (basement), Chaparral Street.

Plate 93:
Unidentified County Office, Old 1919 Nueces County Courthouse, Chaparral Street. Left is Ben Ligon, later district clerk.

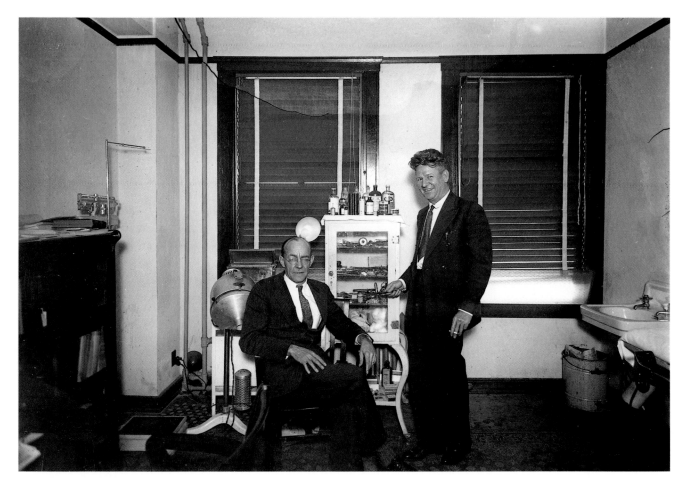

Plate 94: (Opposite, above)
Dr. Bauer, D.D.S., Refugio, Texas.
Pictured here is Dr. Bauer with his
wife, Mary Clair Heard Bauer.

Plate 95: (Opposite, below)
Dr. William H. Gentry with his
receptionist, Miss White, #501
Sherman Building.

Plate 96: (Above)
Examining Room of Drs. Peterson
and Thomson, 207–8 Nixon
Building, (across from the Plaza
Hotel). Pictured here are Dr. O. H.
Peterson (seated), and Dr. Burch
Thompson. This is one of two
photographs the itinerant made of
these doctors.

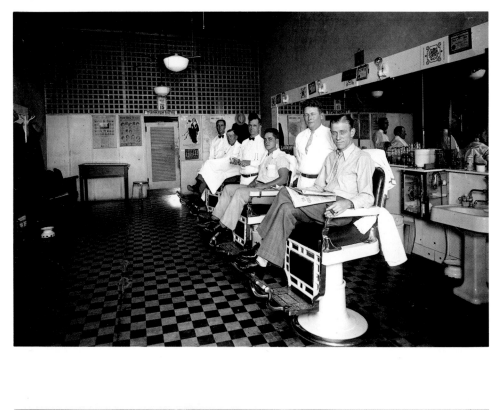

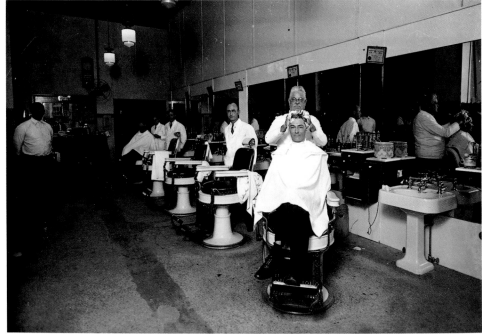

Plate 97: (Opposite, above)
McGregor Barber Shop, 415 Starr Street. The first customer is Jack Taylor, of the Taylor Brothers Jewelry Store (also on Starr Street). The center customer is Valdemar Olsen. The decorative floor tiles indicate that this is a first-class shop. There is a door leading to the turkish baths, a poster illustrating new hairstyles for women, a pinball machine in the rear, and a cuspidor on the floor. Note the pipe arrangement for the first barber's sink.

Plate 98: (Opposite, below)
The Favorite Barber Shop, 311 Peoples Street. Pictured is B. W. Abernathie, owner (standing, right) and Wilson (standing at the second chair).

Plate 99: (Above)
Crow's Barber Shop, 410-A North Chaparral Street. Pictured here from front to rear: Claude H. Crow; J. B. Adams; Perry "Pappy" Crow, president of the barber's union; Jackson, shoeshine.

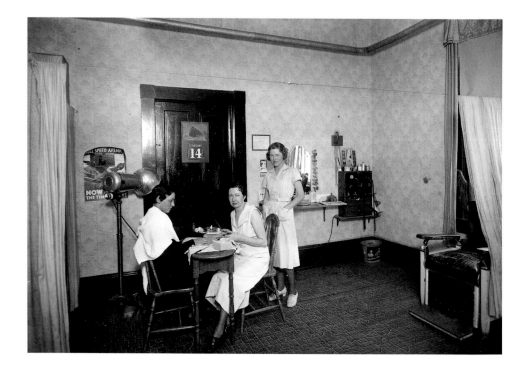

Plate 100: (Opposite, above)
Unidentified Beauty Shop. This shop
had individual booths.

Plate 101: (Opposite, below)
Unidentified Beauty Shop. There is
a license on the wall from the
National School of Cosmeticians.
They used a curtain on a wire and
turnbuckle for a partition. Note the
poster on the wall which reads "Full
Steam Ahead—Now is the Time."

Plate 102: (Above)
Eugene Permanent Wave Shop,
located in the Plaza Apartments,
820 North Chaparral. Note the
signed FDR photograph and the
wooden radio on the left. This shop
was owned by Stella Stinson.

Plate 103:
Royal Tailor Shop, 512 Starr Street. The man shown here used a steam iron with a gas hose connection. The pipe on the wall was a high-pressure steam line.

Plate 104:
Unidentified Dry Cleaner, Corpus Christi vicinity.

Plate 105:
Unidentified Dry Cleaner, Refugio, Texas. This image is remarkably similar to one made in Albuquerque, New Mexico, in October 1930. (See appendix.)

Plate 106:
Eureka Laundry, 1111 Blucher Street, end of Waco Street. Shown here is a press for finishing flatware (sheets and cases) and the overhead line shafts which powered the presses.

Plate 107: (Opposite, above)
Unidentified Hotel. Signs in the
back indicate an upstairs beauty
parlor and a long-distance telephone.

Plate 108: (Opposite, below)
Unidentified Hotel. Pictured on the
left is Porter Parish. The men
seated were salesmen for the Singer
Sewing Machine Agency.

Plate 109: (Above)
*The Princess Louise Hotel, 306
Mann Street, corner of Water Street.*
The nameplate on the counter says:
"L. H. Greer, clerk." Greer is
pictured here. The hotel displayed
timetables for the railroad and bus
routes. This hotel was owned by
Louise and Walter Foster.

Plate 110:
The Plaza Hotel, corner of Upper Broadway and Leopard Street.
Pictured here are Dick Lear (center) and Lonnie Price (left). Lonnie Price is the only person photographed by the itinerant who remembers the photographer. C. W. Pounts was the manager. The Plaza Hotel was a popular gathering place for early south Texas oilmen. The building was demolished in the 1970s from the top down, one floor at a time.

Afterword

Photohistorians fifty years from now will envy us: we have the good fortune to be in the discipline before it has become one. We study and "research" and write, making up rules of inquiry as we go along. We don't work by the book because the book hasn't been written yet.

The golden age of photohistory seems to be over, but the grand old men who created the profession, Helmut Gernsheim and Beaumont Newhall, are still alive and publishing. Thanks to them and other pioneers, a few of the basic assumptions of our trade have been laid down—or so we imagine.

But no one feels constricted. There aren't one or two or several methods that are unavoidable. Any strategy that might help us understand photographs in the richness of their relation to the culture that created and used them is allowed to show its stuff. True, a canon of Reputable Photographers already exists—Gernsheim and Newhall have seen to that. But the canon is charmingly pliant: an important exhibition, a good book, will squeeze a new person in.

Does Sybil Miller's *Itinerant Photographer* get her anonymous hero into the pantheon? I think so. He is to be seen, I suggest, as a kinsman to E. J. Bellocq, doing for Corpus Christi workers and workplaces in the Depression what Bellocq did for the prostitutes of Storyville in the early decades of the century: making them into a record of such visible fineness that we are tempted to use the word *art*.

Though Miller insists her photographer was not an artist, she finds artistic merit in his work. Whether or not you agree with her depends, of course, on what you like and dislike—on your taste and aesthetics (to use a word of critical jargon). I want to discuss something less subjective than taste or artistic judgment. I want to talk about the pictures in this book as cultural artifacts (to use a phrase of anthropological jargon): things made by people that reveal the historical and social context in which they were made.

The poet Randall Jarrell once remarked that two treaties and a bust will give even the worst fool an hypothesis that would take a year to check. This book has lots more information than two treaties and a bust, and even a quick look at its pictures suggests many things about Corpus Christi in 1934. For example:

(1) How formal the time was. The auto parts salesmen look like bankers. Some professional men, wanting to look as distinguished as possible for the camera, wear hats in their own offices.

(2) How informal the time was. These commercial interiors have yet to be rationalized by the ideal of coherent style. Much that we see is still made by hand, and where it isn't, a hand distributes the printed point-of-purchase advertising with such sweet irregularity that the result is cozy and humane.

(3) How visible the heroes of the period were. In the 550-odd interiors in the McGregor Collection, there are nearly a dozen pictures of President Franklin D. Roosevelt, the largest being in a beauty salon (Plate 102). There are several men done up like Charles Lindbergh, with tousled hair, white shirt, short tie, and surprisingly pale pants. There is even a Herbert Hoover look-alike, Abe Klein, the proprietor of a high-class men's clothing store (Plate 37), who has the ex-president's beefy face, pig eyes, and part down the middle of his scalp. Klein is no bitter-ender; he has Roosevelt's NRA—National Recovery Administration—eagle on the wall.

(4) How much Bauhausy streamlined Art Deco had made it into America's hinterland by the early thirties. To me, the most astonishing image in the book is of the drive-up Novo hamburger kiosk, a northern European form deep in the south of Texas (Fig. 1). How did it get there? The first U.S. exhibit of Bauhaus architecture had taken place less than two years before at New York's fledging Museum of Modern Art; can that have furnished the inspiration? Obviously the American provinces then were in closer touch with the rest of the world than we had suspected.

But these are general impressions. Let's look at three specific pictures and see if we can go deeper.

Figure 2 shows a rural barber shop, probably in Woodsboro or Refugio, farm towns in the orbit of Corpus Christi. The men in the chairs are farmhands or cowboys. It is Saturday afternoon, and they have spent the week working in the countryside, with few sanitary conveniences and no

Figure 1.
Novo Drive-In, location unknown.
While this drive-in may have been
located on Corpus Christi's North
Beach, no one has yet been able to
identify it, nor does it appear in any
of the city directories from 1933 to
1935. Since the itinerant
photographer did make at least one
side trip while in Corpus Christi (to
Refugio and Sinton), it is possible
that this picture was made en route
to or from the city.

Figure 2.
Unidentified Barber Shop,
probably in Refugio or
Woodsboro, near Corpus
Christi.

hot running water, maybe no running water at all. They are now getting cleaned up for Saturday night revels and Sunday church.

After their shave and haircut, they will go through the door marked "Baths," have a hot bath, and put on the clean clothes and city shoes or boots they brought with them. The bath will be hot because a hired man, too feeble for fieldwork, will have carried buckets of water from the wood-stove and mixed it with cold water from the tap. After each bath, this man scrubs out the tub for the next customer. He may then wash the work clothes the customer took off and have them ready to be picked up on Sunday afternoon. Some customers may pay to leave their city clothes with the barber from week to week; the hired man will care for them and clean them when they need it.

This photo shows us that, in rural locales only a short while ago, a profession we think we know (barbering) actually involved a good deal more than we had understood. The photographer didn't intend his picture to tell us this: the fact that rural barber shops provided baths and valet service wasn't news to his audience. But we can sometimes learn more from a picture than it meant to say, if we can discover the context in which it was made.

The best way to do this, I think, is the way anthropologists do: through knowledgeable informants. My informants on this picture, without whom

I wouldn't have understood what I was looking at, were Eric Warren and Joe Coltharp, both of whom Sybil Miller acknowledges in her introduction. Joe Coltharp was of particular help. A newsphotographer and, later, the curator of photography in the Humanities Research Center at the University of Texas at Austin, he began life on a ranch and knew exactly what a city boy like me would overlook. He pointed me to Ben K. Green's memoir *Horse Tradin'*, which provides an instructive glimpse of a cowboy's cleaning up for a town weekend in the early thirties.

Plate 6 shows a lunch counter offering a "Dutch Lunch with beer" for twenty cents. This establishment is several cuts above Max and Mame's short-order joint in William Faulkner's *Light in August*, (1932), though we might not feel this were the stools crowded with customers (as in the novel) with hats tilted back on their "inwardleaning heads, smoking steadily, lighting and throwing away their constant cigarettes" while they eat. The counterman in the picture would be a passable casting for Max: mordant, hard-faced, and sly. The counterwoman is too soft and intelligent for "brasshaired" Mame (though in the book Mame, of course, turns out to be unexpectedly soft of heart).

Beer is made much of in the picture—there are four signs for it, and five quart bottles offered as invitations—because it was a novelty at the lunch counter. This is February 1934; Prohibition had ended December 5, 1933, when Utah became the thirty-sixth state to ratify the constitutional amendment repealing it. The mischievous counterman gives beer a salute—tentatively, as if the gesture weren't his idea (as perhaps it wasn't). The counterwoman doesn't join in; it still wasn't ladylike for a southern woman to have her picture taken drinking alcohol, though the flippant ads of the time could show it, as we see. (The picture in the ad was probably done for the national market, which had more tolerant standards of women's behavior than the South did.)

Like Abe Klein's haberdashery, this lunch counter is in compliance with the New Deal's NRA, which reminds us that even Mom and Pop businesses were jawboned into following the NRA codes. All complying enterprises, big and little, were encouraged to display the Blue Eagle ("We Do Our Part"), showing their participation in the collective price rigging.

There is another allusion to the New Deal: the Art Deco machine on the counter bears its name. The machine is just what it looks like, a slotmachine. A push of the lever brings different fruit up; the right combination of fruit wins money. (According to the chart on the side of the machine, the pair of oranges currently up may have paid off.) The pictures in this book show gambling machines on most of Corpus Christi's lunch counters—an unexpected tolerance of a tool of Satan in a state dominated by Baptists and Methodists. But Corpus Christi wasn't your average Texas town; a pleasure port for tourists, it had a Catholic and cosmopolitan past. The city's sheriff at the time, Bill Eliff, didn't care about small-scale gambling, so long as it was "honest" and out in the open.

Figure 3.
*Thomas's Model
Pharmacy, 517 North
Chaparral Street, Corpus
Christi.*

We have learned different sorts of information from the two pictures we've studied so far. The barbershop picture taught us some of the ramifications of the barbering trade in the days before indoor plumbing came to rural America; it told us facts we hadn't known about how certain people *did* things. The lunch counter picture told us about how certain people *felt* about things: beer, women drinking, the NRA, gambling; this is less "objective" information, perhaps, but no less significant.

In Figure 3, the picture of Thomas's Model Pharmacy, Corpus Christi's elite drugstore, contains both sorts of information. Look at the knobs on its soda fountain faucets. The white knobs are for seltzer water or a cola drink. The black knobs are for water, and one black knob is, disconcertingly, on the customer's side of the counter. That black knob shows us one of the ways the South dealt with its climate in the years before air conditioning. When it gets as hot as it does in south Texas, people need to take on water against heat prostration. Those who had ordered something to eat or drink in Thomas's Model Pharmacy (and who, consequently, had a glass in hand) were free to serve themselves as much water as they liked. This spared the soda jerks the nuisance of serving customers who only wanted water refills. It was a thrifty way of being neighborly, and good for the drugstore's goodwill.

The picture shows us, then, something narrow and utilitarian; one way southerners coped with summer. But it also shows us something broad and ideological: what middle-class Americans in the Depression aspired to and how they felt about their lives.

One of the mistakes we make when we look back on the 1930s, those of us who weren't alive then, is to imagine the period in terms of the decade's well-known hardship photographs, which were taken by (among others) Margaret Bourke-White and such Farm Security Administration photographers as Walker Evans, Dorothea Lange, Russell Lee, Arthur Rothstein, and Ben Shahn. These photographs quite rightly appear in our high school and college textbooks and Depression histories because they vividly document the central social reality of the time.

But what they document wasn't the experience of most Americans then. Roosevelt said in his 1936 inauguration speech that one-third of the nation was ill housed, ill clothed, ill fed; two-thirds of the nation, implicitly, was not. Roosevelt—and the decade's documentary photographers—wanted to enlist the fortunate two-thirds of the nation, the middle and upper middle classes, the people who elect and pay for our governments, in a campaign to help the unfortunate third. And, to some extent, Roosevelt succeeded: he was re-elected, his New Deal started many new programs to help the poor.

That the mass of people in the middle class during the Depression voted for candidates who promised to help those suffering from social hardship is the strongest possible proof that Americans of the time were concerned about the poor. But to exaggerate this concern, to say (for instance) that the mass of middle-class people paid attention to social hardship much of the time would be false. The Depression was a period of social concern, as the textbooks say, but the people of the time were people, not saints.

We realize this when we look at pictures like the one of Thomas's Model Pharmacy. Here we see members of the middle class wearing their daily public faces, on moral furlough from concern about the poor. The nonchalant man at center—the store's owner-manager, if my information is correct—isn't thinking about the winter transients in town who, perhaps, rummage in his garbage. That isn't an America he pays much attention to; certainly not the America where his aspirations lie. He and the customers and employees gathered in the slipstream of his power don't identify downward, with the 40 or so million Americans suffering unemployment and deprivation, as the New Deal idealists (and, incidentally, the Communists) would have had them do; they identify upward, toward their social betters.

In the picture these "betters" are embodied by the couple in the candy ad at left. Rich, formally dressed, these people are so far at the top of the heap they can afford to stand around swapping presents (his mints for her smiling attention) and looking good. The woman's insouciant stance, one hand in easy possession of the furniture, is echoed—intensified— in the pharmacy owner's proprietary slouch. We see that he, like a Veblen hero, means to be seen not at work but possessing what he has.

The pharmacy customers (one of them is the manager of the Firestone Tire dealership shown in Fig. 44 of the introduction) and the pharmacy employees emulate the owner. The men copy his gesture, his casual this-belongs-to-me leaning, but with diminishing confidence the farther they stand from his side and status. Both customers and employees are more formally dressed than he: the men wear vests, jackets, hats. In the eyes of those around him, the owner has *arrived:* he can afford to look on holiday, whereas they are still struggling toward the beach.

This picture makes plain a fact overlooked in most writing about American life in the thirties: the people of the time lived in the Depression, but many of them harbored expectations from happier days. Those happier days are embodied in the glossy ad: romantic twenties America; an opulent room; a slick-haired Valentinoid man; a sanitized Theda Bara woman with a bare back, short curled hair, and kiss-me lips.

For the people in Thomas's Model Pharmacy—the slick-haired owner, his employees, and the customers—the 1920s and its promises were not dead. They still aspired to live the American dream of the boom and gain wealth, power in the world, and prestige, not en masse by collective action, but as individuals, thanks to individual initiative.

This picture shows us a Depression face too often forgotten: the face of common people doing well enough for themselves to look forward to doing better.

I suspect photo buffs will compare this book of pictures of people at work in Corpus Christi with the recent *Mining Photographs and Other Pictures: A Selection from the Negative Archives of Shedden Studio, Glace Bay, Cape Breton, 1948–1968*, a book of pictures of people at work in Canada. When it appeared in 1983, *Mining Photographs* caused a stir in photographic circles. It is obvious, I think, that the pictures in *Itinerant Photographer* are livelier than those in *Mining Photographs*. This book hasn't the dour, northern tone of the other one.

What aroused comment about *Mining Photographs* wasn't the pictures but the long, well-written, and deeply committed accompanying essay by photographer and critic Allan Sekula. This essay seems to me to say little that is original, but it has admirable human values—ones given loud voice in a good deal of contemporary art criticism. Sekula praises the workers in Leslie Shedden's pictures for "their solidarity, their resilience, their strong sense of cultural continuity, and their willingness to struggle." I don't see these things in the photographs and don't know how Sekula does, but I share his enthusiasm for them.

I disagree with him, however, when he sees worker pictures as inherently radical. He says that Shedden's pictures of people working or almost working were made at the instigation of company management, which meant to celebrate "teamwork" among the workers and their superiors. He argues that the pictures are in fact subversive of management's intent:

The group photograph . . . harbors another meaning, a meaning that contradicts the logic of management. Here, posed confidently around the instruments and materials of production, are people who could quite reasonably control those instruments and materials. Therein lies a promise and a hope for the future.

That is what Marx thought, said better than Marx said it. But is it true? Couldn't we say that in a real sense the workers in Shedden's pictures, like the workers in this book, *do* control their instruments and materials? They control them quite as much as I control the university ballpoint with which I write these words, which will later be typed on a university typewriter by a university secretary. The secretary is a wage worker, as am I (I will be paid $400 for this essay).

To me, the sadness isn't that others may profit financially from the workers' labors (as I hope others profit from my work here) because the workers are profiting also. The sadness isn't even that the workers aren't profiting *enough*, may deserve a bigger piece of the pie. The sadness for me is the one Paul Goodman pointed out a generation ago in *Growing up Absurd:* that most people in my society and other industrial societies don't have work as rewarding—"manly" was the word Goodman used—as the work (teaching and writing) I have and Sekula has and Goodman had.

But this is perhaps, as perhaps Sekula would say, a bourgeois sadness, since many people, workers and not, wouldn't care to do the kind of work I do, would prefer to do their own work, though it is repetitive and physical.

When Edward Kennedy was running for senator from Massachusetts in 1962, the chief argument against him was that he, at age thirty, had never worked a day in his life. The story goes that one afternoon as he was shaking hands with workers leaving a factory, a midde-aged man asked him if it was true he'd never worked. Kennedy said it was, and the worker responded, "You haven't missed a thing."

We spend one-third of our lives working—more than that if we have to, or are lucky enough to like what we do. Though I love the man for saying Kennedy hadn't missed a thing, I don't agree. I don't think anyone looking hard at these pictures from Corpus Christi will say that work is empty, that none of our human divinity rubs off on it.

Appendix

Albuquerque, 1930. Photographs from the Bandell Collection.

In October 1930, an anonymous itinerant photographer made a series of photographs in Albuquerque, New Mexico, businesses. These pictures show store interiors (and occasionally, exteriors) with the posed owners and employees occupying the center of the frame. They were made on 5×7-inch glass plates, with a wide-angle lens, as were the Corpus Christi photographs made in 1934. The 125 glass-plate negatives that survive today form the Bandell Collection at the Albuquerque Museum, named for the plates's donor, Ray Bandell. Bandell was not a photographer; he received the glass plates in exchange for some carpentry work he did for a local studio photographer, who in turn received them from another, unknown photographer passing through Albuquerque. These circumstances and the materials used by the photographer suggest a connection between the Albuquerque pictures and those from Corpus Christi, a relationship that is reinforced by the pictures themselves.

The Albuquerque photographs tell nearly as much about their maker as the Corpus Christi photographs do about theirs. In the latter, the photographer exhibits a sureness in his handling of craft, materials, and subjects that can only come from extensive experience. The Corpus Christi intinerant obviously had photographed in many other places before he arrived in south Texas. In contrast, the Albuquerque pictures indicate the relative inexperience of their maker. Of the 125 plates in the collection, one was ruined due to double exposure, another because the photographer accidentally pulled the dark slide from the plate holder in bright light, completely exposing one half of the image. In many pictures, the photographer included his shadow in the foreground, perhaps because he was unaware of the intrusion, or perhaps because he found it amusing. (The Corpus Christi itinerant made neither of these mistakes.) To me, the Albuquerque photographer's lack of skill and the careless ruining of at least two plates suggests that he was young and new to the job.

Even with these apparent differences in skill, there are many distinct similarities between the Corpus Christi and Albuquerque pictures, and both groups were made by an anonymous itinerant. Compare, for example, a photograph from Corpus Christi made in a dry cleaners (Fig. 1) with one from Albuquerque made in a combination shoeshine parlor and newsstand (Fig. 2). In the Corpus Christi picture the photographer included the word *Risk* on the left edge of the frame. Since this photographer deliberately used the edges of his photographs in many other instances, we may assume that the placement of *Risk* in this picture was intentional.

In the Albuquerque picture the photographer also placed a significant word on the left edge of the frame—*Murder*. However, the deliberateness of this placement is more ambiguous than in the Corpus Christi pictures. The Albuquerque itinerant, with his relative inexperience, may have consciously placed *Murder* along the edge or he may not have thought much about it. Still, there seems a strong tie between the two pictures.

The connection between the Corpus Christi photographs and those from Albuquerque becomes even stronger when other pictures are compared, such as the Albuquerque photograph of a tire shop (Fig. 10), and the Corpus Christi itinerant's photograph of a dry cleaners in nearby Refugio, Texas (Plate 105). They almost appear to be the same picture, made at about the same time, by the same photographer. Unfortunately, the Albuquerque photographer's identity is unknown, and like the Corpus Christi photographer, he was not newsworthy or memorable. It seems likely that the apparent connection between these two groups of pictures and their makers will never be more than intriguing speculation.

142

Fig. 1:

Unidentified dry cleaners, Corpus Christi, Texas, February, 1934. (Courtesy Harry Ransom Humanities Research Center, University of Texas at Austin; Photography Collection, McGregor Archive.)

Fig. 2:

Buckeye Shining Parlor, 200¹/₂ West Central Avenue, Albuquerque, New Mexico, October, 1930. (All the following photographs were made in Albuquerque, also in October 1930.)

Fig. 3:

Panhandle Refining Company, 1802 North Fourth Street.

Fig. 4:

Unidentified automobile dealer.

Fig. 5:
Unidentified cafe.

Fig. 6:
Unidentified cafe.

Fig. 7:

Unidentified shoe repair shop.

Fig. 8:

New Mexico Motor Corporation, 613-615 West Central Avenue.

Fig. 9:

North Fourth Street
Flour and Feed Mill,
1223 North Fourth Street.

Fig. 10:

Unidentified tire shop.

Fig. 11:

Unidentified barber shop.

Fig. 12:

Unidentified dry cleaners.

Bibliography

BOOKS

American Guide Series. *Corpus Christi: A History and Guide.* Corpus Christi: Chamber of Commerce, 1942.

Chapell, George. *The Itinerant Photographer.* New York: Schoenig and Company, 1936.

Coe, Brian. *Cameras From Daguerreotypes to Instant Pictures.* New York: Crown Publishers, 1978.

Cotner, Robert C.; Robert F. Colewell, Dorothy De Moss, Mary Maverick McMillan Fisher, Merry K. Fitzpatrick, John P. Griffin, Lyndon Gayle Knippa, William E. Montgomery, Marion Martin Nordeman, Diane Treadaway Ozment, Robert Ozment, Bradley R. Rice, Judith Jenkins Turman. *Texas Cities and the Great Depression.* Austin: Texas Memorial Museum, 1973.

Croford, Ava. *The Diamond Years of Texas Photography.* Austin: W. Frank Evans, 1975.

Davenport, Marguerite. *The Unpretentious Pose.* San Antonio: Trinity University Press, 1981.

Gernsheim, Helmut. *The History of Photography: From the Camera Obscura in the Eleventh Century up to 1914.* New York: McGraw-Hill, 1964.

Gilbert, George, ed. *Photo Advertisements A–Z.* Riverdale, New York: Yesterday's Cameras, 1970.

Goldberg, Vicki, ed. *Photography in Print.* New York: Simon and Schuster, 1981.

Harris, Neil. *The Artist in American Society.* Chicago: University of Chicago Press, 1982.

Holt, Paul Glenn. *$50 a Week with Camera and Car.* Boston: R. Snyder, 1926.

Hurley, F. Jack. *Portrait of a Decade.* New York: DeCapo Press, 1977.

Leuchtenburg, William E. *The Perils of Prosperity: 1914–32.* Chicago: University of Chicago Press, 1958.

Newhall, Beaumont. *The Daguerreotype in America.* 3rd rev. ed. Mineola, New York: Dover, 1976.

Parker, Ann, and Neal Evon. *Los Ambulantes.* Cambridge: MIT Press, 1982.

Rudisill, Richard. *The Mirror Image.* Albuquerque: University of New Mexico Press, 1971.

———. *Photographers of the New Mexico Territory, 1854–1912.* Santa Fe: Museum of New Mexico, 1973.

Ryder, James F. *Voigtlander and I in Pursuit of Shadow Catching.* Cleveland: The Cleveland Printing and Publishing Company, 1902.

Slingsby, Robert. *Practical Flashlight Photography.* London: Marion and Company, 1890.

Taft, Robert. *Photography and the American Scene.* New York: Dover, 1964 edition (originally published in 1938).

ARTICLES, MANUSCRIPTS, AND PERIODICALS

Abel's Photographic Weekly (various issues, 1913–31).

Corpus Christi Caller-Times (various issues, 1931–38).

Fischer, Roland G. "H.C. Benke: A Profile; H.C.B. as I Knew Him." Typed manuscript. Madison: The State Historical Society of Wisconsin, Iconographic Collection.

Gorgas, John R. "Reminiscences:" *St. Louis and Canadian Photographer* 23 (1899): 327.

Katz, Leslie. "Interview with Walker Evans." *Art in America* 59 (March–April 1971): 82–89.

Kennedy, Maggie. "A Little Sugar and a Camera and Kids' Dreams Come Alive." *Dallas Times Herald,* December 31, 1980.

Kilgore, Dan E. "Corpus Christi: A Quarter Century of Development, 1900–1925." *Southwestern Historical Quarterly* 75, no. 4 (April 1972): 434–46.

Linton, Edgar. "How I Worked My Way Around the World." *Kansas City Star,* May 26, 1912.

Newhall, Beaumont. "Ambulatory Galleries," *Image* 5, no. 9 (November 1956): 202–7.

———. "Documentary Approach to Photography." *Parnassus* 10, no. 3 (March 1938): 3–6.

Parke, George. "The Tintype Photographer of the Seventies," *Photo-Era* 63, no. 4 (April 1929): 194–95.

Pittman's Trade Tips (various issues, 1930–31).

The Professional Photographer (various issues, 1931–37).

Reardon, Patrick. "History Buff Focuses on America." *The Arizona Republic* (Phoenix), October 3, 1983.

Romer, Grant B. "Letters from an Itinerant Daguerreotypist of Western New York." *Image* 27, no. 1 (March 1984): 12–20.

"Roving Photo Buffs Develop Simple Life with Old Techniques." *Austin American-Statesman,* December 19, 1983.

"Sidewalk Cameramen Snap 70,000—and Keep Snapping." *The Houston Press,* August 26, 1936.

Simpson, Sam F. "Daguerreotyping on the Mississippi," *Photography and Fine Art Journal* 8, no. 8 (August 1855): 252.

Stott, William. *"Documentary Expression* Revisited," *Exposure* 24 no. 1 (Spring 1986): 7–12.

INTERVIEWS WITH AUTHOR

Berlin, Mrs. Dave. Corpus Christi, Texas, June 1982 (taped).

Goldbeck, Eugene O. San Antonio, Texas, October 1982 (taped).

McGregor, Dr. John F. "Doc." Corpus Christi, Texas, Fall 1981.

Price, Lonnie. Corpus Christi, Texas, June 1982 (taped).

Ramirez, Carolyn Williams. Austin, Texas, April 1983 (taped)

Shugart, Mrs. L. A. Jr. Levelland, Texas, March 1983.

Shugart, W. H. Levelland, Texas, Fall 1983.

Smith, Sharon. New York City and Austin, Texas, 1985.

Tallmadge, George Jr. Austin, Texas, Summer 1982.

Tallmadge, Jewell. Corpus Christi, Texas, June 1982.

Talmadge, John Mills. Rockport, Texas, June 1982.

Tinker, Dr. Lorena Jean. Corpus Christi, Texas, June 1982 (taped).

Itinerant Photographer
was typeset by the
University of New Mexico
Printing Plant
in Century Expanded.
It was printed and bound
in Japan by Dai Nippon Printing Company,
by offset lithography in two colors
on Satin Kinfuji.
Dana Asbury edited the book
and Emmy Ezzell designed it.